Depression and Anxiety the Drug-free Way

Mark Greener spent a decade in biomedical research before joining *MIMS Magazine* for GPs in 1989. Since then, he has written on health and biology for magazines worldwide for patients, healthcare professionals and scientists, and is clinical editor for *Pharmacy Magazine*. He is the author of 26 books, including *The Holistic Health Handbook* (2013), *Coping with Thyroid Disease* (2014) and *The Stroke Survival Guide* (2015), all for Sheldon Press.

D0300171
9 781780 334162 3

Overcoming Common Problems

Depression and Anxiety the Drug-free Way

Second edition

MARK GREENER

First published in Great Britain in 2015

Sheldon Press
36 Causton Street
London SW1P 4ST
www.sheldonpress.co.uk

Second edition published 2018

British Library Cataloguing-in-Publication Data
A catalogue record for this book is available from the British Library

ISBN 978–1–84709–485–8
eBook ISBN 978–1–84709–486–5

Typeset by Manila Typesetting Company
First printed in Great Britain by Ashford Colour Press
Subsequently digitally reprinted in Great Britain

eBook by Manila Typesetting Company

Produced on paper from sustainable forests

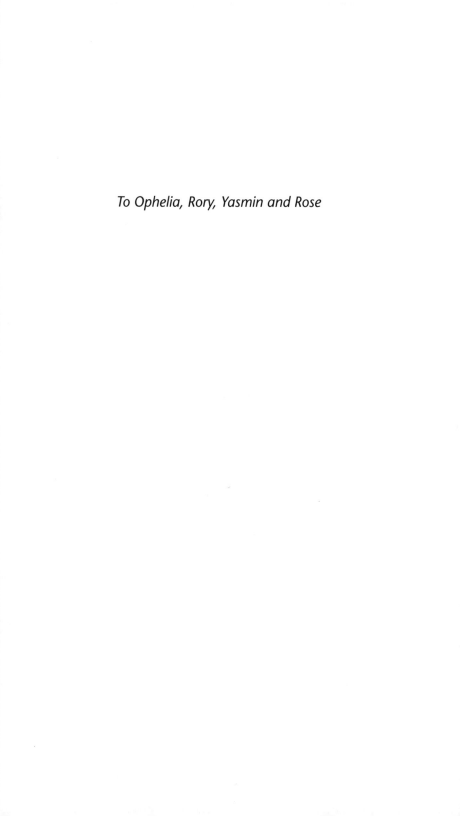

To Ophelia, Rory, Yasmin and Rose

Contents

Introduction

The alarms you just cannot ignore

Depression and anxiety are alarms warning us that something important – mentally, emotionally or physically – is very wrong. Depression and anxiety need to be intense, intrusive and unpleasant: after all, would a gentle, quiet, relaxing car alarm attract your attention? Unfortunately, people with anxiety and depression cannot easily reach the 'off switch'. Living with depression and anxiety is like enduring a car alarm going off day after day, week after week, year after year.

Depression and anxiety rarely have single, easily identified causes. Often mental and emotional layers, in many people laid down since childhood, hide the off switch. Now, several issues, each of which may exacerbate the others, set alarm bells ringing. Overcoming anxiety and depression may mean identifying and addressing each issue, which is not always easy. Meanwhile, each new problem – sometimes, even if relatively trivial – turns the alarm up to deafening volumes.

So, we feel 'on edge' – 'hypersensitive' to life's trials and tribulations. We know that our reactions are often inappropriate or excessive. Yet we cannot control our responses: our emotions control us. Our family, friends and colleagues call us 'grumpy', 'glum' or 'wired'. However, behind these bland, patronizing labels, the pain, distress and discomfort gnaw away at us, damaging relationships with family, friends and partners, destroying careers and contributing to serious physical and psychological problems. Some people find the torment too much to bear and commit suicide.

Depression and anxiety ensnare people as surely as any contraption devised to trap Houdini. However, like Houdini, you can free yourself. You can escape even if you have lived with anxiety and depression for years, even if your problems seem insurmountable, even if you feel the roots lie buried deep in your childhood. Sometimes, following the advice in self-help books (which doctors call bibliotherapy) can alleviate depression and anxiety as effectively as 'talking therapies'.[1] However, reading is not enough: you have to put the advice into action. A book hands you the keys. You need to use them to turn the lock.

A word to friends, relatives and partners

Unless you have experienced full-blown, chronic (long-lasting) depression or anxiety – not just a few days of 'the blues' or 'nerves' – you cannot appreciate how distressing, distracting and debilitating these conditions are. As author and sufferer William Styron commented in *Darkness Visible: A memoir of madness* (see Futher reading), 'to most of those who have experienced it, the horror of depression is so overwhelming as to be quite beyond expression'. So, unless you have been unfortunate enough to suffer depression or anxiety, do not pretend you understand what the person is going through. You don't. If you pretend, a person with depression or anxiety may feel insulted or feel that you are trivializing their torment. However, you can offer, gently and sympathetically, to help.

As personal as your fingerprints

If you break your leg, surgeons look at an X-ray and decide the best way to fix the fracture. If you have a heart attack, cardiologists use a battery of tests to suggest tailored treatments that dramatically increase your chances of survival and reduce the risk of another attack. If you have a bacterial infection, doctors give you an antibiotic that usually eradicates the bug.

Occasionally, doctors find a physical cause for depression and anxiety. Ailments as diverse as thyroid disease, obesity, stroke and diabetes can provoke or exacerbate depression and anxiety.[2] Having diabetes roughly doubles the chance of developing depression, for example. The relationship runs both ways. Pain and other physical symptoms that you shrug off when you feel relaxed seem more intense and take on more sinister hues when you feel depressed or anxious. Even if a disease does not directly cause psychological problems, anxiety or depression undoubtedly makes you feel worse.

Usually, doctors cannot identify a physical cause for depression and anxiety and they cannot run tests to guide treatment, although there are promising signs that this might be possible in the future. Your depression and anxiety is as personal as your fingerprints. Your specific combination of environment, circumstances, biology and personality underlies your risk of developing depression and anxiety, the causes and how well you respond to treatment.

Drugs are only part of the answer

Doctors cannot write a prescription for a pill that eradicates depression and anxiety the way analgesics eradicate pain or antibiotics eradicate bacterial infections. As depression and anxiety rarely have a single cause, tackling the condition usually means devising a personalized, multifaceted, holistic approach that works for you. You might combine medicines, lifestyle changes and the 'talking therapies' (psychotherapy), for instance. If your symptoms are mild or you suffer a low mood between 'bouts' (the technical term is 'in remission'), lifestyle changes alone might be enough to make you feel better or prevent the problem from getting worse. Lifestyle changes – such as exercise[3] – and psychotherapy[4,5] are often as effective as medicines for mild to moderate depression and anxiety. Indeed, according to the National Institute for Health and Care Excellence (NICE), psychotherapy is usually the treatment of choice for mild to moderate depression and anxiety.

Nevertheless, access to psychotherapy varies around the country, which partly explains why GPs in England alone wrote almost 65 million antidepressant prescriptions during 2016, according to the NHS. That's more than double the 31 million prescribed in 2006. Yet antidepressants and anxiolytics (drugs for anxiety) only paper over your psychological cracks. You might feel better for a while – but the cracks remain and often just get worse. Over time, the cracks can lead to emotional, physical and mental subsidence – often when you are least able to cope.

As Kirsch comments in *The Emperor's New Drugs: Exploding the antidepressant myth* (see Futher reading), 'the belief that antidepressants can cure depression chemically is simply wrong'.[6] Indeed, antidepressants may exacerbate your problems. For instance, antidepressants can blunt both ends of your emotional spectrum. You may be less likely to descend to the depths of depression. However, you may also feel less able to experience peaks of pleasure. So, antidepressants lock some people into a world of reduced pleasure and happiness. This perpetuates their need to take antidepressants.[7] After all, being unable to enjoy activities you previously found pleasurable (which doctors call anhedonia) is an important hallmark of depression. Meanwhile, withdrawal symptoms can make it difficult to stop taking antidepressants and anxiolytics. Ironically, withdrawal reactions include anxiety and depression – the conditions the drugs were supposed to help – possibly locking you into a cycle of debilitating symptoms.

Nevertheless, when you have severe depression and anxiety, tackling deep-seated problems can be difficult, if not impossible. It's all you can do to keep going. Sometimes you cannot even manage that. You lack the drive to tackle simple issues. You feel frozen by fear. Some people find that antidepressants and anxiolytics take the edge off their symptoms, offering a breathing space that allows them to deal with the underlying issues. Drugs are a ladder against the wall of the prison of anxiety and depression. They can help you escape. But you won't get far without other support on the other side. You'll just hang around waiting to be recaptured.

A word of warning

Never stop taking *any* medicine – including anxiolytics or antidepressants – without speaking to your doctor first, even if you feel better. Suddenly stopping some anxiolytics or antidepressants can provoke severe withdrawal reactions (page 44), including dizziness, unpleasant sensations (such as 'electric shocks'), headache, irritability, insomnia, nightmares and disturbing changes in perception. *Always speak to a doctor before you stop antidepressants and anxiolytics or reduce the dose.*

Underestimated, underdiagnosed and undertreated

Every seven years, the government funds the Adult Psychiatric Morbidity Survey in England. The 2014 survey found that 1 in 6 (17 per cent) of people aged 16 years and older reported experiencing a common mental disorder in the week before being interviewed. One in 30 (3.3 per cent) suffered depression and 1 in 17 (5.9 per cent) generalized anxiety disorder (GAD).[8] As we'll see, people with GAD are the classic worriers. They experience 'free-floating', excessive anxiety about several threats and, typically, develop physical symptoms (page 24).[9] In addition, almost 1 in 25 people experienced phobias (2.4 per cent), obsessive compulsive disorder (OCD; 1.3 per cent) or panic attacks (0.6 per cent).

Women were more likely than men to experience a common mental disorder. Indeed, just over a third of men (35.19 per cent) and half of women (51.2 per cent) reported that they had experienced a common mental disorder at some point. A fifth of men (20.0 per cent) and a third of women (34.5 per cent) had been diagnosed by a healthcare professional as suffering from a common mental disorder.[8] The difference between the two figures implies that a considerable amount of suffering is never brought to the attention of a healthcare professional. Indeed, according to the Adult Psychiatric Morbidity Survey, about 40 per cent of people with depression are not receiving treatment. Overall, just 11.8 per cent of people with common mental health problems reported receiving psychological (talking) treatments.

Despite being common and despite the millions of prescriptions written each year, depression and anxiety remain underestimated, underdiagnosed and undertreated. For example, GPs correctly recognized and diagnosed just 34 per cent of GAD cases.[9]

Jackie's story
Jackie, a middle-aged account director, has suffered bouts of anxiety and depression since adolescence. Once, when she went to her GP with crushing depression, and almost terrified from panic attacks and GAD, the doctor told her to have a cup of tea and a biscuit when 'she felt a little upset'. 'It would be funny if it wasn't tragic,' Jackie said.

This book aims to help you help yourself. We will look at the different types of depression and anxiety, some common causes, as well as conventional and complementary treatments. We will not look at anxiety and depression in children and teenagers, bipolar disorder (previously called manic depression) or depression or anxiety after giving birth (postpartum or postnatal). The causes, consequences and treatment differ.

Depression and anxiety tell us something is profoundly wrong with our lifestyle, circumstances or relationships. Don't ignore these warnings. Don't suffer in silence. Anxiety and depression are devastating for the person and, often, partners, family and friends. I hope this book will inspire you to make the changes, and get the help you deserve, to switch off those incessant alarms.

A word to the wise

This book does not replace advice from doctors, nurses, therapists or pharmacists, who tailor suggestions, support and treatment to your circumstances. See a doctor if you feel unwell, think that your signs, symptoms or the impact on your life is getting worse or you are worried that you are have developed side effects or withdrawal reactions.

A massive amount of research has examined the causes, consequences and treatment of anxiety and depression, and it's impossible to cite all the papers, websites and books I used. (Apologies to anyone whose work I have missed.) The articles referenced are a starting point if you want to know more.

Some papers may seem rather erudite if you do not have a medical or biological background. Do not let this put you off: they are usually understandable if you do some background reading and ask questions. You can find a summary of the available papers by entering the details of what you are looking for here: <www.ncbi. nlm.nih.gov/pubmed>. Some full papers are available free online and several publishers offer patients relatively cheap access. Larger libraries might stock or allow you to access some better-known medical journals. The better informed you are, the better you will be able to free yourself from the shackles of depression and anxiety.

1

Don't dismiss depression

Depression can be rational, logical and appropriate. Is it any wonder that a person who loses a partner who shared their life for decades becomes depressed? Or that a loyal, hardworking employee who is coldly dismissed during a 'corporate restructuring' develops melancholia? Or a person with a disabling, life-threatening disease has bouts of tearfulness?

Such trials and tribulations are part of being human. That so many people *do not* descend into depression or succumb to anxiety when facing serious physical or mental illnesses, injury or adversity, amazes me. Some people even manage to use their adversity as a springboard to personal growth. Unfortunately, not everyone shares their mental, physical and emotional resilience. The interactions between environment, circumstances, biology and personality mean that some people develop debilitating depression when facing 'normal' life events.

Depression is much more intrusive and distressing than the low mood many people experience at difficult times. Depression is a profound, debilitating mental and physical lethargy, and leaves the person unable to enjoy once pleasurable activities (anhedonia). Depression is a pervasive sense of worthlessness, despite evidence to the contrary. Depression is an intense, deep, unshakable guilt and crushing sadness.

Depression is even different from the deep, distressing emotions people face when they grieve for a close friend or relative (page 65). 'Compared to depression, the blues I felt when my father died was like someone gently stroking the back of my hand', one person who had endured several bouts of severe depression told me. 'Depression is like being hit in the nose and teeth by a heavyweight boxer.'

Depression *is* a disease

Just because some people overcome seemingly insurmountable problems calmly and with a smile *does not* mean that depression is your

A common problem

Estimates of the number of people who develop at least one episode (bout) of major depression (page 6) during their life vary widely – from about 3 per cent to 40 per cent of women, and up to approximately 30 per cent of men – partly depending on the population studied. Depression seems to be less common in Asian countries, for example.[10] However, some cultures may manifest emotional and physical suffering by developing physical rather than mental symptoms (page 8), which makes determining the number of people with depression difficult.

fault, that your symptoms signal moral turpitude or divine retribution, or that you are weak. Depression is as much a disease as influenza, heart attacks or leukaemia. Depression and anxiety can be just as upsetting, just as difficult to live with, just as distressing as some physical diseases and disabilities. Yet depression and anxiety do not typically engender the same 'sympathy', help and support.

To make matters worse, myths, misconceptions, stigma and ignorance surround anxiety, depression and other mental illnesses. For example, family, friends and colleagues, sometimes with the best of intentions, tell someone with depression, 'Pull yourself together'. But people with depression may be unable to muster the motivation, sense of purpose and confidence to 'pull themselves together' even though they desperately want to. Depression leaves many people listless and indecisive, and erodes self-esteem. So, they have to push themselves – often very hard – to work or perform other 'everyday' activities that other people take in their stride. Mustering the energy and motivation to work, or look after children, can drain their resources leaving too little to allow them to help themselves.

Many people with depression also live with considerable anxiety (see Chapter 2). In one study, almost 7 and 11 per cent of men and women respectively reported *both* anxiety and depression.[9] In another study, 34 per cent of people with major depression (see below) had one of the various forms of anxiety.[11] For example, some people in remission become anxious about whether their depression will return. In others, the combination of environment, circumstances, biology and personality that led to depression triggers anxiety and vice versa.

Depression's core symptoms

While the causes, symptoms and treatment of depression differ from person to person, doctors recognize several core symptoms. These are not unique to depression, which can complicate diagnosis. For example, people with depression typically spend considerable time ruminating (brooding and obsessing) about the past. They feel guilty about mistakes, times when they let others down, and events and acts that they regard as immoral or sinful. They may ask constantly, 'Why does this happen to me?' Rumination, Tacchi and Scott note, can mean that people become depressed about being depressed.[176] However, excessive, inappropriate guilt can be a symptom of several other mental illnesses including anxiety, OCD (page 29) and bipolar disorder.

Table 1.1 overleaf lists examples of depression's core symptoms, and the more of the symptoms listed you have, the more likely you are to have depression, especially if they persist and interfere with your day-to-day life. So, see your GP as soon as you can if you have little interest or take little pleasure in doing things you used to enjoy, or you feel down, depressed or hopeless for most of the day, every day for more than two weeks. See your doctor *urgently* if:

- you feel that life is unbearable;
- you are considering or taking steps towards suicide or self-harming (page 19);
- you are unable to meet your work, social and family obligations;
- you hear voices in your head, which are usually critical or defamatory, or experience visual hallucinations. Hallucinations can be symptoms of a very serious condition called psychotic depression.

Do I have depression?

According to NICE, answering 'Yes' to either of the following questions suggests that you might have depression and should seek professional help.

- During the last month, have you often been bothered by feeling down, depressed or hopeless?
- During the last month, have you often been bothered by having little interest or pleasure in doing things?

Table 1.1 Depression's core symptoms

Psychological symptoms of depression

Considering suicide, self-harm or taking steps towards suicide
Continuous low mood or sadness
Feeling anxious or worried
Feeling hopeless and helpless
Feeling irritable and intolerant of others
Feeling ridden with guilt – especially if the guilt is excessive or unjustified
Feeling tearful or crying
Lack of interest in things or activities – especially if these were once important or enjoyable
Lacking motivation
Low self-esteem
Procrastination – finding it difficult to make decisions

Physical symptoms of depression

Change in appetite or weight (weight usually decreases, but may increase)
Changes to the menstrual cycle
Constipation
Feeling lethargic – moving more slowly than usual
Lack of energy
Loss of libido
Sleep disturbances – such as finding it hard to fall asleep at night (takes more than about half an hour) or early-morning waking
Speaking more slowly or less than usual
Unexplained aches and pains

Social symptoms of depression

Avoiding contact with friends and family
Avoiding social activities
Neglecting and not being interested in your hobbies and interests
Poor performance at work (e.g. poor concentration, lack of motivation and absenteeism)
Problems in your home and family life

Source Adapted from NHS Choices <www.nhs.uk>

The duration of depression

Depression waxes and wanes. Some people recover completely between episodes (bouts) of depression. Others endure milder residual symptoms (page 49). Each episode of major depression (see below) typically lasts between four and eight months.[176] In one study, half of people with major depression recovered within 3 months, while

63 per cent recovered within 6 months.[11] Although scientists have investigated depression's triggers extensively, they are less sure of why people recover. Often depression abates without a dramatic change in the person's life.[12]

Some people, however, experience symptoms for considerably longer: in the study mentioned above, 24 per cent had not recovered from an episode of major depression after a year; about 20 per cent still experienced depression after two years.[11] Typically, a severe bout of depression tends to last more than twice as long as an episode of mild or moderate depression. Not surprisingly, many people with depression feel that they will never recover. They become 'depressed about depression',[6] which further hinders recovery.

About 25 per cent of people with depression experience only a single episode, often after a traumatic life event, such as unemployment, divorce or bereavement. However, on average, a person with depression experiences between four and eight episodes. About 60 per cent of people who recover from an episode of depression experience a recurrence within five years.[13] Depression seems, however, to be especially persistent in older people. For instance, a study of 1042 people found that a diagnosis of depression was still present after two years in 36 per cent of people aged 18–29 years compared to 51 per cent of those aged 70 years or older. Furthermore, 18.2 per cent of those aged 18–29 years had a chronic symptom course compared to 40.6 per cent of people aged 70 years or older.[205] You can take steps between episodes to bolster your resilience – our ability to adapt effectively to stress, problems and adversity – and reduce your risk of recurrence.

Rating your distress

Doctors cannot take a blood sample to diagnose depression or use brain scans to find the cause. They cannot evaluate an antidepressant's effectiveness based on measurable changes – as they can assess antihypertensives based on reductions in blood pressure. So, your GP will probably use a 'rating scale' – essentially a scientifically validated questionnaire – to diagnose depression, assess severity and track your response to treatment.

Many doctors use the Hamilton Depression Rating Scale. You can find online versions, but you might need a doctor's help to interpret the results. Doctors will listen to you describe your symptoms (try keeping a diary – page 7) and look at your behaviour – your facial expression, posture, voice, whether you cry, wring your hands, bite

A nervous breakdown

A 'nervous breakdown' is not a medical term, but it describes a real problem: a sudden inability to function from day-to-day due to stress, anxiety or depression. You can suffer a nervous breakdown when life's demands overwhelm you physically, psychologically and emotionally. You may be unable to go to work. You may avoid social engagements and miss appointments. You may have trouble eating, sleeping and coping with personal hygiene. A nervous breakdown is an unequivocal sign that you need help.

your nails or lips, and so on. If your distress is severe enough or your score crosses the rating scale's threshold, doctors diagnose 'major depression'. Below this threshold, doctors diagnose 'minor' (also called subthreshold) depression, which is often anything but.

Doctors will also assess severity. According to NICE, mild depression just crosses the threshold (such as number of symptoms) for diagnosis. The symptoms have only a minor impact on the person's life. People with severe depression have many more symptoms than those with mild depression. Importantly, the symptoms 'markedly interfere' with the person's ability to function. Moderate depression falls between these extremes.

Between 5 and 16 per cent of people attending GP surgeries seem to have minor depression.[14] While these people do not reach the threshold for full-blown depression, they feel much more miserable, more critical of themselves and less able to deal with 'everyday' demands and problems than people without depression. However, because the symptoms are milder, some lifestyle changes suggested later in the book may help without resorting to antidepressants. If this applies to you, you may find that the lifestyle changes may also bolster your resilience so that minor depression does not develop into the full-blown condition. This is important as between 10 and 25 per cent of people with minor depression develop major depression within 1 to 3 years.[14]

The many faces of depression

Depression expresses your distress. So, depression can take many forms. Sometimes, depression's symptoms emerge so gradually that

Table 1.2 Symptoms of atypical and melancholic depression

Symptoms of atypical depression

Increased appetite or marked weight gain
Excessive sleep or sleepiness
Leaden paralysis (arms and legs feel too heavy to move)
Profound fatigue
Abnormal sensitivity to rejection by other people

Symptoms of melancholic depression

Reduced appetite
Early morning waking
Depression that is worse in the morning
Psychomotor retardation (slowing down of thought and movement) or agitation
Excessive guilt

Source Adapted from Edwards,[15] Lasserre et al.[16]

Keeping a diary

You could keep a diary ranking each of your physical, mental and emotional symptoms on a scale of zero (absent) to 10 (the most severe you can imagine or have experienced). This will help your doctor diagnose your problem, understand whether physical symptoms are part of the depression (page 8) and track your response to treatment. Note any possible triggers (such as what you were doing when the symptom flared) and the impact on your quality of life and day-to-day activities.

Even if there is nothing to report, complete the diary each day for a month or so (or two to three months if symptoms emerge less frequently; for example, for women who experience depression or anxiety around the times of their periods). It's often difficult to recall how bad you felt several months later and a diary can show that you are making progress. A diary might also suggest that you are beginning to feel worse and, perhaps, you will be able to take steps to avoid a full-blown attack. You can also jot down your worries, concerns and issues, which can help you find a path out of your problems. Remember, you don't need to show this part of the diary to anyone, unless you want to.

the person does not notice. They struggle on adjusting their lifestyle to cope. Eventually small changes accumulate into a major impact. Some people realize that something is wrong only after a friend or relative highlights how much their appearance or behaviour have changed. Depressed people often lack the motivation to take as much care with their personal appearance or health and fitness as they did in the past.

In other cases, depression emerges suddenly, with or without an obvious trigger. The speed of onset and the relationship to a trigger can vary in the same person. One episode may emerge slowly after a stressful event. Another event may trigger a rapid decline. On other occasions, the person may be unable to link their bout of depression to a particular event. The pattern of symptoms can also vary between people and in the same person over time. For example:

- people with 'atypical depression' tend to overeat, oversleep, feel profoundly fatigued and are extremely sensitive to rejection; women tend to show atypical depression more often than men;[15]
- people with melancholic depression tend to undereat, wake early in the morning and feel guilty.[16]

Table 1.2 compares these two types of depression to show how varied the condition can be.

When depression hurts the body

Spilling hot tea in your lap hurts. Looking at photographs of your ex can leave you feeling another kind of pain. The experiences may seem distinct, yet many languages describe social rejection in terms of physical pain.[1] Recent studies suggest that the description is more than metaphorical: the brain regions that are active when you experience physical and emotional pain overlap.[200, 201] Indeed, about two-thirds of people with depression develop physical (also called somatic) symptoms.[17] Indeed, some people with depression find that physical, rather than psychological, symptoms predominate. Doctors call this 'somatization disorder' or 'masked depression'. Typical symptoms include:[15, 18]

- aches and pains, which often seem to be 'everywhere' rather than in specific places such as muscles or joints;
- back pain, especially in the lower back;
- breathing difficulty or breathlessness;
- chest pains;

- digestive problems, such as nausea, diarrhoea or constipation, and stomach pain;
- dizziness, light-headedness or feeling faint;
- headaches;
- problems swallowing;
- tiredness, exhaustion and fatigue.

These can be symptoms of potentially serious physical diseases including heart disease, malignancies and asthma. So, see your doctor if you experience any of these symptoms even if you think that they might be caused by depression.

For some people, somatic symptoms offer a 'socially acceptable way of indicating emotional distress'[18] and often emerge when the person has difficulties expressing the true depths of their feelings.[15] Strikingly, for instance, some people who witnessed the torture and horrors of the Cambodian killing fields reported fuzzy vision or even blindness, yet doctors could find nothing medically wrong with their eyes.[19]

Culture and society influence the pattern of somatic symptoms. A UK man with depression may complain of headaches, fatigue, or aches and pains. He is unlikely to complain that his penis is retracting into his body. However, a vanishing penis is 'a perfectly acceptable symptom in Malaysia and South China'.[20] Chinese people also typically complain of somatic symptoms in their liver, spleen, heart or kidneys. People in Iran and the Punjab tend to experience somatic symptoms that affect their heart.[18]

Some people refuse to believe that physical symptoms could arise from their mind. So, they blame their symptoms on rational, if mistaken, causes, such as a virus, abuse or chemicals. Other people may believe in bizarre causes, such as a conspiracy to poison the water, satanic abuse or alien abduction.[20] Effective treatment depends on identifying, and the person accepting, the 'true' cause.

Dysthymia

About 6 per cent of us live with dysthymia – chronic mild depression. The symptoms of dysthymia are less intense than in major depression, but they persist for longer and do not disappear for more than two months at a time. Dysthymia's symptoms include:

- anger and irritability;
- difficulty making decisions;

- feeling guilty;
- feeling pessimistic and hopeless;
- feeling unable to cope with the demands on you;
- insomnia or oversleeping;
- loss of interest in daily activities and avoiding social activities;
- low energy, tiredness and fatigue;
- low self-esteem, being self-critical;
- poor appetite or overeating;
- poor concentration.

Although milder than major depression, dysthymia can still dramatically undermine quality of life and relationships. Partners, for example, may complain that you are 'cold' and 'distant'. Friends, relatives and colleagues may describe you as 'miserable' and 'grumpy'.

About three-quarters of people with dysthymia develop major depression during the next five years.[15] People who suffered dysthymia in the past also seem to recover more slowly once they develop major depression. In one study, on average, an episode of depression lasted about 14 months in those with dysthymia compared to 8 months in those without.[11]

Seasonal affective disorder

Many people prefer the summer to autumn and winter, but for between 3 per cent and 5 per cent of the population, declining light levels as summer turns to autumn trigger a type of depression called seasonal affective disorder (SAD). People with SAD develop many of the core symptoms of depression (see Table 1.1), including excessive sleepiness, lack of energy and fatigue, lack of interest, pleasure and motivation a tendency to overeat (especially carbohydrates, which encourages weight gain), difficulty concentrating and withdrawing from social activities.[177] People with very severe SAD can stay in bed all day or even attempt suicide. Many more people experience milder SAD. According to a YouGov survey of 2031 people, commissioned by the Weather Channel (Table 1.3):

- 8 per cent of UK adults interviewed reported full-blown SAD;
- 29 per cent experienced some SAD symptoms, but did not have the full-blown condition;
- 57 per cent said that their overall mood is worse in the winter than the summer;
- 66 per cent said their mood in the winter makes them feel less active.

Table 1.3 The proportion of people with symptoms that could indicate SAD

Symptom	Experienced symptom in the winter (per cent)	Sought medical advice or treatment during the winter (per cent)
Fatigue	40	6
Low energy levels	39	4
Greater need for sleep	36	3
Weight gain	30	3
Greater appetite	27	1
Low self-esteem	14	3
Stress or anxiety	16	8
Increased desire to be alone	11	2
Trouble concentrating	7	2

Source Adapted from a YouGov survey of 2031 people commissioned by the Weather Channel

The SAD season lasts, roughly, from October until mid April. If you experience low mood or SAD – or your depression gets worse – during the winter, here are some suggestions that might help.

- Try to spend at least 30 minutes a day outside. Exercising is ideal: physical activity alleviates SAD and depression more generally (page 99). If possible, roll up your sleeves and expose your skin to sunlight, but avoid getting sunburnt.
- Let as much natural light into your home and work as possible. Open curtains and blinds.
- Make sure you get enough vitamin D (page 77), which might mean taking a supplement.
- Try taking St John's wort, which some people find helps (page 116).

If these suggestions don't make you feel better, you could buy a light box certified as a medical device for SAD. You will need, for example, to sit close to the light box for two 30 to 45 minutes sessions a day, once in the morning and once in the evening. Some manufacturers allow you to try the light box before you buy it. If you are not sure, ask your doctor or the Seasonal Affective Disorder Association. If lifestyle changes and light therapy do not adequately alleviate your symptoms, you might want to consider medicines or complementary therapies. Many people find that treatment is most effective in the early morning. Most people respond within 1 to 3 weeks.[178] Side effects of light therapy can include eye strain, headache, agitation, nausea and sedation.[178] Interestingly, some people with non-seasonal depression and bipolar depression also seem to benefit from bright light phototherapy.[177]

Depression's elusive cause

Essentially, depression arises when the demands on a person outstrip their physical and mental resources. Indeed, one or more stressful life events seem to precede about four of five episodes of major depression.[21] Your personal combination of environment, circumstances, biology and personality determines your resilience and, in turn, whether you cope or develop depression. Numerous studies underscore the intimate link between stress and depression.

- In one study, 68 per cent of people with depression had endured a very stressful life event or experienced 'highly unpleasant' major difficulties that had threatened their plans, goals and aspirations during the previous year. Just 18 per cent of people without depression experienced major problems over the same time.[22]
- In an Australian study, work-related stress increased the risk of depression or anxiety by 54 per cent. Personal stress increased the risk by 70 per cent.[23]
- American researchers found that 90 per cent of 'burnt out' teachers were depressed. Of these, 92 per cent crossed the threshold at which doctors usually suggest drugs, psychotherapy or both. Of those with depression, 63 per cent had atypical symptoms. Emotional exhaustion was more strongly associated with depression than reduced personal accomplishment, both core features of burnout.[24]
- Debt increases the risk of common mental disorders, such as anxiety and depression, almost three-fold, according to a study from England. Of those in debt, 38 per cent had at least one common mental disorder compared to 14 per cent of those without debt. Debt roughly doubled the risk of depression.[25]
- Many single mothers, especially those on welfare and who live in socially and economically deprived areas, develop depression.[15]

Stress isn't always bad

Despite the link to depression, anxiety, suicide and other mental health problems, stress isn't always bad. You need a certain amount of stress to crawl out of bed in the morning. Many actors, musicians and people making presentations welcome 'stage fright': the heightened arousal enhances their performance. Horror film aficionados delight in the frisson of fear, which they find cathartic.

'Stress' describes our level of arousal. As we become more aroused, our senses become more acute, we mobilize more energy and our mental abilities sharpen. That is why too little stress can lead to boredom, apathy and poor concentration, which can also cause depression and anxiety. However, too many of us have too much of a good thing. Over-arousal – what most people mean by 'stress' – undermines performance. You feel 'stressed out' when the demands on you increase your arousal to a point that outstrips your resources, resilience and time.

When a performance, presentation or movie ends, your arousal normally declines. However, people with depression and anxiety often remain on edge – so-called hyperarousal. Your body will begin to tell you that you are overdoing it. When physical symptoms emerge, when you drink alcohol excessively, when you begin to feel the first signs of a bout of depression or anxiety, it is probably time you took stock and recharged your batteries.

Locus of control

Apart from triggering depression, stress seems to undermine the effectiveness of antidepressants and psychotherapy, and makes a relapse more likely. However, your view of the trigger is important. Stress is more likely to trigger depression when you regard the problem as uncontrollable, unpredictable and severe, and feel you cannot cope.[26] For example, a company's most stressed-out employees tend to be those working long hours in repetitive jobs for low pay, with little control over their work: production-line workers, checkout assistants, call-centre staff and so on. One analysis that looked at 38 studies that evaluated the links between stress and mental disorders – such as anxiety, depression and suicide – found that:[27]

- people with limited opportunities to take decisions were 21 per cent more likely to develop a mental health problem than those with more control;
- people who experienced poor relationships at work were 32 per cent more likely to develop mental health problems;
- people who felt there was a marked discrepancy between the effort they put in and their reward were 84 per cent more likely to develop mental health issues.[27]

If work causes or makes a large contribution to your depression, it is time to consider your employment and retraining options. (Try the problem-solving tips on page 66.) When you cannot change the trigger – when depression is the legacy of redundancy, bereavement or divorce, for example – you can change your response. However, this depends on feeling that you control circumstances, rather than that circumstances control you.

Psychologists describe the extent to which you feel you control your life as your 'locus of control'. A strong internal locus of control means you tend to see yourself as in charge of your life. If you have a strong external locus of control, you see yourself as having little influence over your life. You feel that events control you. As a result, people with an external locus of control react worse to stress than those with an internal locus of control[26] and are especially prone to developing anxiety and depression. As we see later, you can nurture an internal locus of control, which is a keystone of your resilience.

In some cases, numerous low-level, persistent difficulties trigger depression: the accumulation of problems wears the person down. Depression may recur because problems, and stress, ebb and flow. So, improving your ability to recover from daily stress – such as by active relaxation (page 113) – may cut the risk of a recurrence. Remaining positive, identifying the various problems and then deploying effective approaches to cope can improve your resilience and reduce the chances of another episode.[28]

Depression's childhood roots

Not surprisingly, perhaps, adolescence's trials and tribulations can cause depression. Estimates vary, but 8 per cent to 20 per cent of adolescents develop major depression.[204] Indeed, people with depression often trace the roots of their distress to neglect, abuse or maltreatment during childhood. When researchers combined results from 16 studies, maltreatment during childhood roughly doubled the risk of recurrent and persistent depression among adults. Adults with depression who were maltreated as children were also 43 per cent more likely to respond poorly to treatment than people who were not abused.[13]

Children have few defences against physical, sexual and emotional maltreatment by people that they should be able to trust. Adults – and stronger peers – can impose their will physically, emotionally and psychologically. Bullying typically occurs at a vulnerable time in our emotional and psychological development. In other words, bullying can alter the 'trajectory' of the victim's life course. Indeed, victims often carry the burden for the rest of their lives. One study looked at studies examining the mental health of adolescents (11–19 years) with depression when they were aged 21–35 years. Of 18 articles, 17 showed that adolescent depression increased the risk of experiencing the condition as an adult almost three-fold. Seven of eight articles found that adolescent depression increased the risk of adult anxiety up to eight-fold. Three of five articles reported a link between adolescent depression and adult suicidality.[204]

Maltreated children defend themselves by, for example, repression and denial (page 55). They do not learn the effective coping strategies that other people use to defend themselves against the problems they face as adults. So, as adults they're more likely to use unhelpful coping strategies when faced with problems (page 54). Maltreatment even can alter the way the brain is connected. People who were maltreated as children are 'hardwired' to be more sensitive to stress and, in turn, prone to anxiety and depression.

Maltreatment and bullying undermine academic performance: it's difficult to focus on lessons if you live haunted by the spectre of beatings at home or in the playground. So, maltreatment and bullying may reduce the victim's chances of getting a good education. As adults, maltreated and bullied children may experience problems sustaining their attention or regulating their emotions. This, of course, hinders their ability to hold down a job. As a result, they are more likely to face financial and relationship problems, which further exacerbates stress, and, in turn, their risk of developing depression and anxiety.

Sometimes even adults might not realize the extent of the abuse they endured when they were children, especially if the maltreatment was predominately emotional. After all, they had little to compare their upbringing with: many maltreated children are withdrawn with few if any friends, even as adults. As we'll see (page 105), good relationships with family and friends are important defences against stress and depression. Also, the maltreatment was 'normal' for these survivors, which can result in them passing the torch of depression to their children.

We learn many parenting skills from our mothers and fathers. So, a person who was maltreated as a child may not have the skills they need when they face the challenges of raising their own children. One man with a long history of depression, who was physically and emotionally maltreated by his parents and severely bullied at school, told me that when he faces a difficult situation with his kids, he thinks what his mother and father would have done in similar circumstances. Then he does the opposite. Based on his happy and well-adjusted children, who are now teenagers and adults, it seems to have worked.

In other words, childhood maltreatment can cast a long shadow over the rest of the person's life and even beyond. Understanding the causes – counselling and psychotherapy can help – allows you to come to terms with a traumatic childhood, move on and leave your depression behind.

Genes and depression

Depression can run in families, in part because of the shared environment, in part because we learn coping strategies from our parents, and in part through our genes. Overall, genes seem to account for about 38 per cent of the risk of developing depression. However, genes account for between 48 and 75 per cent of the risk of developing severe depression that needs hospital treatment[29] and for at least half of your response to antidepressants.[30] In the future, doctors may analyse your genes to tailor treatment more effectively and predict your prospects more accurately.

You cannot change your genes – although researchers are working on 'gene therapies' for several serious diseases that involve changing the genetic code. However, 'rewriting' the genetic code for depression

Understanding your genes

Almost every one of your 10 trillion cells contains an 'instruction manual' to make your entire body, encoded in DNA's famous double helix. The amount of DNA in your body almost defies belief. Pulled into a single, microscopically thin strand, your DNA would go from the earth to the sun and back more than 300 times, or wrap around the earth's equator 2.5 million times.[31]

In humans, DNA is tightly wrapped into 23 chromosomes that contain the 25,000 or so genes that make you 'you'. These genes determine the colour of your eyes and hair, your features and influence your chances of developing certain conditions, including depression. You get almost half your genes from your father. Mitochondria – the cell's powerhouses – have their own genetic code. This circular genome contains 37 genes and always comes from your mother. So, you get just over half the total DNA from your mother.

is many years away from routine use, partly because several genes seem to contribute to the risk of depression and the patient's response to treatment. In the meantime, you can tackle your environment, circumstances and other non-genetic factors that account for up to two-thirds of the risk of developing depression.

Depression and chemical changes

Antidepressants' commercial success – supported by pharmaceutical companies' marketing budgets – led to an emphasis on chemical changes in the brains of people with depression and anxiety. As we will see in Chapter 3, antidepressants alter levels of some chemicals in the brain. However, these chemical changes do not seem to cause depression.[6] Biologists do not yet understand the chemical and nervous pathways that link stress to depression's emotional and behavioural symptoms.

Biologists no longer believe that the brain's wiring is unalterable. Your nerve circuits adapt as you learn new tricks, skills and facts. For instance, during pregnancy, a mother's brain shrinks by around 4 per cent to meet the baby's demands for energy. Mothers recover the loss within about six months of giving birth.[32] Rehabilitation after a stroke or injury allows new parts of the brain to control the body, which helps overcome the disability.

Trauma (including, as we have seen, childhood maltreatment) can change the organization of the network of nerves in the brain, which leaves a person more vulnerable to stress and, in turn, depression. Indeed, brain scans show reductions in the sizes of parts of the brain that control emotion, mood and cognition in people with depression,[33,34] which contribute to persistent and recurrent depression. Brain scans are also beginning to identify different patterns in people who respond well to antidepressants and psychotherapy.

So, the chemical changes are, probably, the consequences, rather than the causes, of depression. After all, alcohol alleviates social phobia (sometimes called social anxiety disorder) – severe anxiety when you feel yourself to be the centre of attention (page 28). However, a lack of alcohol in your body does not cause social phobia. Alcohol does not correct a chemical imbalance in the brain that causes social phobia.[35] The same principle applies to depression and antidepressants.

Depression and physical diseases

Almost every disease our flesh is heir to can trigger depression in certain people. Sometimes, a touch of depression is a good thing: depression following pain and injury might reduce movement, which helps prevent further damage. Depression might 'force' you to take things easy for a while, which offers your body the chance to recover physically.

More usually, however, depression can make you feel worse, hinder your chances of making a full recovery and may even prove fatal. For instance, depression increases the risk of death during the six months after a heart attack by around four-fold.[36] A stroke survivor with depression is three times more likely to die in the 10 years after the stroke than a survivor without depression.[37] Depression seems to increase the risk of death after a stroke or heart attack, in part, by reducing the person's engagement with, and motivation about, treatment. Therapists helping the rehabilitation of people who survived a stroke or heart attack may pick up depression when the person does not improve as expected or shows, for example, poor concentration or motivation.

The relationship between depression and physical disease runs both ways. Here are some examples.

- Depression increases stroke risk by about 34 per cent, partly beacuse depressed people are more likely to smoke, drink alcohol heavily, eat unhealthy diets and be physically inactive than those without a low mood.[38]
- Depression increases the risk of developing diabetes by 60 per cent.[39] Diabetes seems to double the likelihood of experiencing depression.
- Depression increases the likelihood of obesity (page 83) by 58 per cent. On the other hand, obesity increases the risk of developing depression by 55 per cent. Even being overweight, rather than obese, increases the risk of depression by 27 per cent.[40]
- Depression increases the likelihood of developing dangerously raised blood pressure (hypertension) by 42 per cent.[41]
- A third of people with Parkinson's disease show depression. In about 30 per cent of people with Parkinson's, depression pre-dates the hallmark movement symptoms.[42] The changes in the brain that lead to Parkinson's also seem to trigger depression.
- Chronic pain sufferers are four times more likely to suffer depression or anxiety than the general population.[43] People can also experience chronic pain as a somatic symptom of emotional distress.

There is not enough space to consider all depression's links with physical ailments. So, raise any concerns you have that a physical disease might cause or contribute to your depression with your doctor. Looking for physical causes is especially important when depression arises for the first time in elderly people.[15] Physical ailments are more likely to cause depression as you get older. Treating the physical disease may alleviate the depression.

As you get older, however, you're more prone to developing physical diseases that also need treatment. Researchers have linked more than 200 medications to an increased risk of depression or suicide, including some beta blockers and certain other antihypertensives (used to reduce blood pressure), proton pump inhibitors (used to reduce acid in the stomach), as well as a number of painkillers and hormonal contraceptives. Proton pump inhibitors and oral contraceptives, for example, seemed to double the risk of depression in older people and starting antidepressants respectively. The risk is especially higher in people taking least three medicines linked to depression. About 1 in 7 people (15 per cent) of these developed depression compared to 1 in 20 (4.7 per cent) of those not taking any such drugs.[206] So if your depression recurs or gets worse after starting a new medicine, speak to your doctor or pharmacist.

The dangers of overshadowing

Doctors can become 'fixed' on one problem and ignore other explanations – so-called diagnostic overshadowing. A person with depression can develop chest or bowel symptoms that a doctor may 'dismiss' as somatization (page 8), but that could indicate asthma, heart disease or gastrointestinal cancer. The best way to overcome diagnostic overshadowing is to give the doctor a full picture of your symptoms (you could keep a diary, for example) and insist that you are sure that your depression or anxiety does not cause the problem.

Watch for suicide and self-harm

Tragically, many people with depression find that life becomes too much to bear and commit suicide. Many more self-harm to punish themselves or express their distress – perhaps as a cry for help (Table 1.4). Self-harm can also relieve tension and provide a sense of control over situations that people feel they cannot otherwise influence. Sadly, many people seem to feel this way: according to the Institute of Psychiatry, one in ten young people in the UK self-harm. Furthermore, about 40 per cent of people with depression experience suicidal tendencies at some point.[15] Indeed, the risk of suicide is some 15 to 20 times higher in people with depression or bipolar than in the general population.[176]

The stages of suicide

Suicide typically develops in four stages.

1 Initially, people think about suicide almost philosophically – so-called 'passive suicidal ideation'.
2 Then, people move to active suicidal ideation. During this stage they think about the suicide's impact on their family and friends, and consider how, when and where to kill themselves. This may include researching methods of suicide.
3 The person prepares to act. They may write a will, give away their possessions, write letters and place their affairs in order.
4 Finally, they make the attempt.[47]

However deep your suffering, remember that, as psychologist David Bresler remarks, 'suicide is a permanent solution to what might very well be a temporary problem' and 'if you act on these thoughts, you won't be around later on to change your mind'. Even these 'simplistic and obvious' statements often provide 'profound food for thought for those considering suicide and its consequences'.[47] It's easy to lose sight of even the simplistic and obvious in the depths of depression or anxiety.

> ### Excoriation disorder
>
> Up to 1 in 50 people show excoriation disorder – a compulsion to pick at their body, usually faces, arms and hands. Between 57 and 100 per cent of people with excoriation disorder have a psychiatric problem, usually anxiety or depression. However, excoriation disorder typically precedes anxiety or depression. Behavioural interventions specifically targeting skin picking are the most effective treatments for excoriation disorder. Treating depression or anxiety alone generally does not resolve skin picking.[46]

Stanley's story

Stanley remained at the 'passive suicidal ideation' stage for years: he found the philosophical contemplation reassuring. He knew that if the pain became too much there was an 'escape route'. However, when he lost his job, he began actively researching the least painful way to kill himself, and gave away and sold his beloved collections of books, videos and CDs. He persuaded himself that, financially, his family would be better off without him and that his depression was causing a rift with his wife, who would soon leave him. Over a few weeks, he collected the medicines he planned to overdose on. Thankfully, the thought of his suicide's impact on his young children forced him to reconsider. 'I worried it would sow the seeds for depression in their later life,' he said. 'I wouldn't wish my depression on my worst enemy'. His wife reassured him that she had 'no intention of going anywhere'. He no longer indulges in the philosophical contemplation: 'It's the first step on a dangerous road'.

Table 1.4 Types of self-harm

Banging or hitting head, such as on a wall, table or hard with hand

Deliberate burning or scalding

Deliberate gassing

Deliberately swallowing hazardous (e.g. corrosive or caustic) materials or substances

Deliberately swallowing inedible objects

Deliberately taking an overdose of medicines, street drugs; sometimes alcohol abuse is a form of self-harm, especially when mixed with other substances

Excessively scouring or scrubbing the body

Hair pulling – the Ancient Greek physician Hippocrates remarked that stress leads some people to tear their hair out, a condition now called trichotillomania[45]

Watch for the warning signs

If you find yourself in any of the four stages of suicide, seek help from a doctor, helpline, counsellor or a religious leader. If you are a relative or friend of a person with depression or another mental illness, always take suicidal tendencies or suicide talk seriously. Do not dismiss any of the following warning signs as attention seeking:[15]

- a period of agitation and then calm, as this may reflect the torment of making the decision to commit suicide; then a sense of peace once the decision is made;
- a worsening of depression and hopelessness;
- changing a will;
- direct and indirect threats of suicide;
- discussing or preparing for suicide;

- giving away possessions, especially if valued or sentimental;
- isolation and loneliness;
- viewing websites about suicide.

While you always need to remain vigilant, certain people are at increased risk at certain times, such as after the death of a loved one, after divorce, unemployment or legal problems. A study from 26 European Union countries found that each 1 per cent increase in unemployment increased suicide rates among people younger than 65 years by 0.79 per cent.[48]

Furthermore, most suicide attempts occur in the first three years of suffering depression.[15] The longer you endure depression and anxiety the better you learn to cope, such as by avoiding situations likely to trigger problems. This may help cut the suicide risk. Suicide risk may rise in the early stages of drug treatment for depression (page 43). So, you and the people around you need to be especially vigilant for changes in thoughts or behaviour that could be linked to self-harm or suicide.

If you feel you are suicidal or even feel that you are getting to the end of your tether then see your GP, go to A&E or phone a helpline such as:

- Samaritans – 116 123;
- Breathing Space – 0800 838587;
- HOPELineUK – 0800 068 41 41 (see the Useful addresses at the end of the book).

Suicidal ideation, talk and attempts, as well as self-harm generally, are loud shouts for help. These helplines offer advice, support and comfort. They can help stop you making a decision you might not live long enough to regret.

2

The many faces of anxiety

Sometimes, anxiety is prudent. Anxiety produces physical, mental and behavioural changes that warn us of, and help us deal with, potential dangers, such as walking alone late at night. However, if anxiety or its milder counterpart, worry, nags away at you, you probably should deal with the trigger. As Tallis notes in *How To Stop Worrying* (see Futher reading), 'worry is like an alarm system that tells you it's time to deal with a problem'.

Anxiety disorders arise when our natural 'fear' reaction is out of proportion to the threat or is excessively prolonged. Being terrified by finding a 15-centimetre (6-inch) Brazilian Wandering Spider in your supermarket bananas is prudent. The Wandering Spider produces one of the most deadly arachnid venoms. Being terrified by a money spider is a phobia.

About a fifth of adults experience an anxiety disorder at some time.[49] In a survey for the Mental Health Foundation in the UK, 29 per cent of those interviewed said that anxiety and fear had stopped them from doing things they wanted to – and these were people who did not meet the medical criteria for full-blown anxiety.[179] Essentially, people with anxiety are highly sensitive to potential threats. Their enhanced fear response leaves them 'hyperaroused' and sensitive. They may endure excessive and inappropriate fears about, for example, losing their job, road accidents and being attacked. They may imagine how things could get worse: it's easy to create a cascade of problems arising from a trivial issue that lead to devastating consequences. People with anxiety fear the worst, making it difficult to take decisions even to alleviate their distress.

Anxiety can take many forms, from focused phobias to a generalized vague sense of danger. Psychiatrists call these the 'anxiety spectrum disorders'. People with post-traumatic stress disorder (PTSD) and obsessive–compulsive disorder (OCD) share similar symptoms to 'classic' anxiety disorders. Some psychiatrists now consider PTSD and OCD as separate to anxiety disorders.[49] Nevertheless, they are closely related and we'll consider them later.

When anxiety goes awry

Anxiety increases mental alertness and heightens the acuity of your senses to help you detect danger early. Adrenaline and other chemicals flood your body. So, your heartbeat becomes more rapid, which means blood reaches your muscles more quickly. Indeed, the amount of blood reaching muscles may increase by 1,200 per cent.[179] You breathe more rapidly. You sweat. Blood flows from your skin and your intestines to your muscles – that's why we go pale when we are extremely stressed or frightened. As your body dramatically reduces digestion, you produce less saliva. That's why fear leaves you with a dry mouth.[179] Muscles surrounding the hair follicles tighten – that's why we get goose bumps. Our pupils dilate so more light reaches the eye[179] – that's why we're wide-eyed with fear. Many of these changes – wide-eyed, flared nostrils and raised eyebrows, for example – seem to allow us to see and smell better, which helps our survival.[179]

These changes are part of the 'fight-or-flight' response, which evolved to get us out of trouble quickly with the least possible damage. The fight-or-flight response was a lifesaver when our ancestors faced a rival tribe on the warpath or hungry carnivorous animals. Unfortunately, the 'fight-or-flight' response does not distinguish between barbarian hordes and a pile of final demands, or between a sabre-toothed cat and a nagging boss.

The natural response when facing fear is to get and remain somewhere safe. So, people with anxiety often avoid situations that trigger anxiety or make sure they can escape, for example, by sitting close to

Hormonal changes

Many organs release or respond to hormones and other chemical messengers. For example, your adrenal glands, which lie on top of your kidneys, secrete several hormones – including adrenaline, noradrenaline (called epinephrine and norepinephrine respectively in the USA) and cortisol – that take part in the fight-or-flight response. These messengers, for instance, raise heart and lung activity, and slow digestion. They also release fat and glucose to fuel our muscles and other organs. Meanwhile, your brain produces natural painkillers to help you fight or escape even if you are injured.

a door. Fear focuses on the future[179] as people prepare to cope with events they fear might be negative, unpleasant or dangerous. Depending on the trigger, people with anxiety may avoid flying or social situations, even though this damages their career prospects and hinders their leisure activities. However, because they adapt their lifestyles, many people with anxiety never receive the help they need, which usually means psychotherapy (see Chapter 4) rather than anxiolytics. These 'safety behaviours' also mean that they don't discuss the fears and realize they are unfounded, which perpetuates the anxiety.[179]

The many forms of anxiety

Doctors diagnose anxiety when 'fear' symptoms are prolonged or excessive, cause significant distress or hamper your social or daily life.[49] Anxiety can take several forms, the most common of which are listed below.

- Generalized anxiety disorder (GAD): free-floating anxiety about several threats, usually accompanied by physical symptoms.[9]
- Obsessive–compulsive disorder (OCD): recurrent, distressing or pointless thoughts and impulses that the person cannot ignore; performing a compulsion dissipates the anxiety.
- Panic attacks: sudden, intense, overwhelming fear accompanied by marked physical symptoms. People with panic attacks worry that they will lose control, become embarrassed or even die.[15,21]
- Phobias: fear of an object, place, situation, feeling or animal that is out of proportion to the risk. Almost anything can trigger a phobia including: peanut butter sticking to the top of your mouth (arachibutyrophobia); being without a mobile phone (nomophobia); stickers (pittakionophobia); and thunder and lightning (tonitrophobia, among several other names). However, for people with these conditions, the phobia is no joke.
- Social anxiety: severe anxiety when a person feels that they are the centre of attention, such as speaking in public, working in a group and even signing a document or a cheque. Some psychiatrists regard social anxiety as a type of phobia.
- Illness anxiety: excessive or disproportionate preoccupations with having or acquiring a serious illness.[49] People with this type of anxiety may fear, for instance, that a minor ache is the first sign of cancer, or 'pins and needles' is the first sign of multiple sclerosis.
- Separation anxiety, which can affect adults as well as children.

Anxiety disorders and suicide

Anxiety dramatically increases the risk of suicide and self-harm (page 19). For instance:

- agoraphobia (fear of situations where escape might be difficult or help would not be available) without panic disorder increases suicidal ideation between five- and eleven-fold and suicide about four- or five-fold;
- GAD increases suicide ideation between three- and eight-fold and suicide around five- or six-fold;
- panic disorder with or without agoraphobia increases suicide ideation between four- and six-fold and suicide about five-fold;
- PTSD (page 31) increases suicide ideation about five-fold and suicide around seven-fold;
- social anxiety disorder increases suicide ideation and suicide between four- and five-fold;
- specific phobias increase ideation about three-fold and suicide around three- or four-fold.[50]

People with anxiety disorders and their friends and relatives should watch for the warning signs of suicide (page 21).

You can have more than one anxiety disorder. A person with a severe zoophobia may endure panic attacks when they face animals. Anxiety can also cause physical symptoms: being 'sick with fear', having 'the runs' or complaining of 'butterflies in the tummy'. Anxiety also causes tense muscles; strong, fast or irregular heartbeats; 'pins and needles'; shortness of breath and hyperventilation. Stroke survivors, for example, may experience panic attacks during which they hyperventilate, which they may mistake for another stroke. Even health-care professionals can mistake panic attacks for stroke, heart attacks or asthma exacerbations.

Generalized anxiety disorder

People with GAD are excessively and inappropriately anxious about *several* (rather than one or two) potential unrelated threats,[51] for example, unemployment, road accidents and violence. Anxiety about personal safety alone, for example, is more likely to arise from PTSD or agoraphobia than GAD. People with GAD may even worry excessively and inappropriately about trivial matters, such as not doing the housework for a day or two, being a couple of minutes late, or their day-to-day performance at work. They're the classic 'worriers'. To make matters worse, people with GAD may worry about worry. They may worry that their worry is a sign of insanity,[179] especially as people with GAD often realize their concerns are excessive or unfounded.

People with GAD usually recognize that their anxiety is excessive and inappropriate. Yet the intensity means that, untreated, GAD can undermine work performance, relationships and leisure activities. GAD also worsens outcomes for several physical diseases and increases the risk of depression, alcohol abuse and even suicide.[9,51] A study found that, in England, for example, 29 to 62 per cent of GAD patients have major depression and 38 per cent abuse alcohol.[9]

Nevertheless, people with GAD typically do not seek help for many years. Some seek medical attention only after depression emerges following several years of trying to cope with GAD or because they want relief from GAD's physical symptoms.[51] On average, people seem to live with GAD for at least 20 years. GAD only occasionally resolves without treatment.[52] So, the sooner you get help, the better your prospects. Speak to your doctor, counsellor or psychotherapist.

Do I have GAD?

Answering yes to either of the following questions suggests that you might have GAD.[9]

- During the past four weeks, have you been bothered by feeling worried, tense or anxious most of the time?
- Are you frequently tense, irritable and having trouble sleeping?

Phobias

We all know people who are terrified of seemingly innocuous objects, places or animals. (Despite its use in everyday speech, a phobia isn't a dislike or mild fear. Phobias bear the same relationship to mild fear or dislike as depression does to 'feeling a bit down'. Phobias are often debilitating and disruptive to normal life.) A money spider, harmless snake, or standing on a secure first-floor balcony surrounded by a high railing may trigger intense anxiety, and even panic attacks, in people with arachnophobia, ophidiophobia and acrophobia, respectively. Sometimes, just thinking about the trigger provokes a panic attack.

According to the British Psychological Society, specific phobias centre on a single object, situation or activity – such as snakes, enclosed spaces (claustrophobia), vomiting (emetophobia) or choking (pseudo-dysphagia). The so-called complex phobias involve several *related* anxieties. (This is different to GAD, where the anxieties are unrelated.) For instance, people with agoraphobia may fear open spaces, crowds, public places, travelling on public transport and other situations where they are unable to escape home or to another place of safety.

People who have a phobia try to avoid the feared object, situation or activity. When confronted with the trigger most phobic people develop mild anxiety. However, some people experience severe anxiety and even a panic attack. In about 1 in 100 people, agoraphobia causes severe distress and significantly limits daily activities, for example. Phobias are common, as the following examples show.

- The British Psychological Society says that about 1 in 20 adults has agoraphobia.
- According to NHS Choices, about 1 in 10 people experience claustrophobia at least once in their lifetime.
- According to NHS Choices, up to 2 people in 100 have panic disorder. About a third of these will develop agoraphobia.

Exposure therapy (page 61) is one of the most effective ways to deal with a phobia. You confront your fears in safe and controlled situations. The fear gradually subsides as you become accustomed to the trigger.

Social anxiety disorder

Estimates of the number of people with social anxiety disorder (sometimes called social phobia) vary widely, partly depending on how the disorder is diagnosed. NICE notes, however, that social anxiety disorder is one of the most common anxiety disorders and might affect up to 1 in 8 (12 per cent) of people some time during their lives. Indeed, up to 1 in 14 (7 per cent) of us might experience social anxiety disorder in any year.

Social anxiety disorder is more than shyness. Those with it expect to seem, Freeman and Freeman note, 'foolish, inadequate, or unintelligent' to other people.[179] Rather than focus on the task – giving a presentation, for example – they focus on their failings. Yet these views bear little resemblance to reality and are 'often widely distorted and brutally unkind'.[179] After a social event, for example, those with social anxiety disorder may perform a post-mortem that focuses inevitably on any perceived failings rather than what went well. Their impression is often markedly different from that of their colleagues and other people.

Many people with social anxiety disorder, which typically begins in adolescence or early adulthood, have low self-esteem, fear criticism and may have a particular issue with authority figures. No one likes being regarded poorly by people we would like to see us in a good light or who influence our future. However, most people have sufficient self-esteem and confidence to shake off criticisms and weigh up negative evaluations accurately. People with social anxiety disorder do not have these defences and take criticisms to heart. If a harassed, preoccupied-looking boss sweeps past in a corridor, most people would assume he or she has a lot to think about. A person with social anxiety disorder may feel he or she is being deliberately ignored, feel rejected and even worry that the boss is going to fire him or her.

Interpersonal therapy (page 62) can help people with social anxiety disorder socialize, and look and feel more confident. Medicines called beta blockers (page 52) can reduce some physical symptoms if, for example, the anxiety mainly arises around giving presentations. People with social phobia often find relaxation techniques useful (page 113).

Obsessive–compulsive disorder

Many of us have mild obsessions and compulsions – such as repeatedly checking that we locked the front door or car, or having cupboards that have to be organized in a certain way. These may seem excessive. But they do not really interfere with our daily lives or cause profound anxiety. However, around 1 per cent of us have a more serious condition called obsessive–compulsive disorder (OCD).

People with OCD experience recurrent thoughts or impulses, which are typically aggressive, sexual or religious. They recognize that the thoughts are senseless, inappropriate or excessive. Yet if they try to ignore them, they can experience anxiety, which may be intense. People with OCD attempt to get rid of the anxiety by completing repetitive, time-consuming, purposeful behaviours or actions (compulsions). They feel intense anxiety if they do not perform the compulsion.[15]

For example, those obsessed about contamination may have the compulsion to clean repeatedly,[49] sometimes washing their hands up to 50 times a day, until their skin is raw. They may avoid situations that can trigger obsessions, such as shaking hands. Other people with OCD become distressed if things are not in a particular order or keep every receipt and official document often from many years ago 'just in case I need it'. OCD usually develops gradually, beginning in adolescence. The symptoms then wax and wane. If a ritual affects your life or causes marked anxiety, seek advice and support from a doctor, counsellor or psychotherapist.

Panic attack disorder

Each year, 1 in 50 of us experiences at least one panic attack:[49] a sudden, intense, oppressive fear that overwhelms rational thought. MIND notes that a panic attack is an exaggeration of the body's normal reaction to excitement or stress. However, there is often no obvious trigger, or the reaction is out of proportion to the stimulus. For example, panic attacks can arise when a person believes that a normal feeling – palpitations and a tightness in the chest, for example – may mean they are suffering a heart attack. But anxiety can also trigger, for example, a racing heart and breathlessness, which traps you in a cycle that's hard to break.[179]

Your heart may pound 'fit to burst' during a panic attack. You may sweat, feel faint and tremble. You may feel that you cannot breathe or are choking. Your limbs may shake. You might experience chest pains, nausea or dizziness, and tingling sensations. Your vision may blur or swim. Symptoms usually peak within 10 minutes and subside after 5 to 20 minutes. Panic attacks can leave you feeling weak, exhausted and sometimes with lingering anxiety.

A panic attack is terrifying – even if you know what to expect. You may experience only one or two attacks, perhaps when you face a particular phobia, challenge or difficultly. However, according to MIND, some people have one or more attacks a month or even several times each week. Not surprisingly, people with regular panic attacks worry that they will lose control, black out, become embarrassed, or even die. So, they may avoid situations and places where coping or escape would be difficult.[15,21]

You might identify a cause: people with phobias and social anxiety disorder may experience panic attacks when confronted with their triggers. However, panic attacks can strike randomly. As MIND remarks, nocturnal panic attacks can be especially distressing. You may wake confused and, as you were asleep, nocturnal panic attacks strike without warning.

Fearful spells

Some psychiatrists refer to 'fearful spells' – distressing bouts of anxiety that do not cross the threshold for panic attacks. However, people with fearful spells are up to four times more likely to develop several full-blown disorders including panic disorder, agoraphobia, GAD, social anxiety disorder, alcohol abuse and dependence, major depression and dysthymia.[53] In other words, fearful spells offer an early warning. So, try to relax, watch your caffeine (page 94) and alcohol intake (page 89) and consider counselling (Chapter 4).

Post-traumatic stress disorder

PTSD is common after sexual assault, physical attack or military combat. For example, UK reservists deployed to Iraq in 2003 were around 2.4 times more likely to develop PTSD during the next five years than those who remained at home.[54] PTSD is also common in people with a serious physical or mental illness. Around a quarter of people who suffer acute coronary syndrome (heart attacks and a related condition called unstable angina) develop PTSD.[55] Up to 35 per cent of cancer survivors have PTSD. Up to 86 per cent experience some PTSD symptoms, but do not cross the threshold for the full-blown disorder.[56]

People with PTSD often report flashbacks that emerge 'out of the blue' and vivid dreams and nightmares about the trauma. They typically avoid places and people that evoke memories of the trauma, refuse to speak about their experiences and feel constantly on guard or emotionally numb. PTSD can place a considerable strain on relationships, and increases the risk of suicide, drug and alcohol abuse, and aggression. A study from the USA found that about a third of veterans of the Iraq and Afghanistan wars had contemplated suicide (32 per cent), had been physically aggressive, such as threatening people verbally or with a weapon, or being involved in a fight (32 per cent), or had alcohol-related problems (34 per cent).[57] So, seek professional help.

Separation anxiety

People with separation anxiety experience marked fear or anxiety when away from, for example, their home, partner, children and sometimes pets. They may persistently worry about potential harm to their child, relative or partner.[49] Other people mooch around the house when their partner or children are away. Missing your partner, children or pets is not, of course, abnormal. Indeed, some psychologists believe that anxiety and sadness when you are separated from family and friends help maintain social ties.[179, 180, 181] However, if the anxiety and distress become excessive and start affecting your life, then you might want to consider seeing a counsellor or psychoanalyst.

Separation anxiety is relatively common among children. However, adults also experience separation anxiety manifest as, for example, over-strict parental controls, deep jealousy or marked trouble sleeping when away from a specific person. Children who experienced separation anxiety may be more likely to develop panic disorder when they are older.

The causes of anxiety

Worrying about your loved ones, taking precautions against infections, or feeling frightened when a doctor tells you that you have a serious disease is natural. However, separation anxiety, phobias and PTSD are exaggerated responses.

Your personal combination of environment, circumstances, biology and personality determines whether you develop anxiety and the form it takes. Environmental causes include too much caffeine (page 94), abuse of certain street drugs, some physical diseases, withdrawal from antidepressants (page 44) and alcohol.

Again, genes (page 16) account for about 20 to 40 per cent of the risk of developing anxiety.[179] Indeed, we seem to inherit a predisposition to some styles of thinking – such as regarding ambiguous situations as potentially dangerous or being very sensitive to the changes in the body (such as heart rate and breathlessness).[179] These styles of thinking can lead to anxiety. Genes may also account for 30 to 40 per cent of the risk of developing a phobia. The influence of your genes seems to be stronger for animal phobias than agoraphobia.[58]

Circumstances also strongly influence the risk of developing anxiety. For instance, being in debt was found to increase the risk of social anxiety (page 28) and phobias about four-fold, increase the risk of panic disorder more than three-fold and double the likelihood of OCD and GAD.[25]

Gaps between expectation and reality can cause anxiety and depression. For example, housewives in the 1950s who felt that they were 'locked' into stereotypical roles often experienced anxiety.[59] After all, the First World War and the Second World War had shown that women were more than capable of doing 'man's work'. Even today, advertising, celebrity 'stories' and reality TV tend to engender unrealistic expectations about life, possessions and relationships. Advertising often aims to create expectations and stimulate desire, sometimes by evoking envy, jealousy, avarice and other counterproductive emotions. And any similarity between reality TV and the reality of the lives most of us lead is purely coincidental. However, if you take these things seriously or uncritically and let them seep into your subconscious, the inability to have everything we want, or counsels of perfection in life and relationships, can cause anxiety and depression. Attempts to bridge the gap can also lead to debt, which, as we have seen, commonly triggers or exacerbates anxiety and depression.

Parents as a cause of anxiety

The roots of anxiety can reach back into your childhood. Bullying, conflict between parents, sexual and physical abuse and the death of a parent all make anxiety in later life more likely.[179] Our parents strongly influence our chances of developing anxiety through their genes and behaviour. As Tallis comments in *How to Stop Worrying* (see Futher reading), 'parents provide children with example behaviours that tend to be copied. If we grow up in a family where it is normal to "expect the worst", then it is quite likely that we will grow up "expecting the worst" too'.

Similarly, some parents teach their children that we live in a dangerous, hostile world. This might be understandable, especially if they live in parts of the country where violence is a real threat. But some parents become overprotective. This means that the child may not learn to cope with the problems.[179] Other parents strongly disapprove or punish children when they make a mistake, so children become overcautious.

You can learn phobias: children may fear spiders or a storm if their parents live with arachnophobia or astraphobia, respectively. Again, this makes sense: many animals teach their young when to be wary. Such behaviours become 'automatic'. Fortunately, psychotherapy (Chapter 4) can help you relearn these entrenched lessons.

Physical diseases and anxiety

Anxiety can cause or exacerbate several physical ailments. For instance, GAD seems to increase the likelihood of gastrointestinal, cardiovascular (heart and blood vessels), hormonal and respiratory (lung) disease. Patients and healthcare professionals may focus on the physical symptoms, which, augmented by the stigma surrounding mental illnesses, often means GAD goes undiagnosed and untreated.[9]

As with depression, the relationship runs both ways. Around 20 per cent of stroke survivors experience anxiety,[60] which may emerge several months after the stroke.[61] Anxiety seems to arise from damage to parts of the brain that regulate emotions caused by the stroke, the challenges of living with a disability or both. Speaking to your care team may help you access different aids and therapies that may help reduce the disability and, therefore, alleviate the anxiety. In other words, whether you think your anxiety might arise from a phobia you developed in childhood, a physical ailment, or you cannot identify a cause, try the self-help tips and if these do not work, see a doctor, counsellor or psychotherapist.

3

Medicines aren't the answer

At first sight, depression treatment has come a long way since healers in the fifth century BC suggested smoking cow dung to treat melancholia.[62] In the seventeenth century, healers used a mix of rhubarb, senna and myrobalans to treat anxiety – by purging the bowels. As we've seen, gastrointestinal somatic symptoms are common in people with anxiety. Others used tobacco and opium as tranquillizers.[12] During the early twentieth century, psychiatrists tried a chemist shop's worth of drugs as antidepressants including chloral hydrate – the main ingredient in the 'knockout' drink known as a 'Mickey Finn'; barbiturates; amphetamines; and, for agitated people, morphine. They also investigated, with varying success, insulin comas, chemical and electrical shocks, and 'sleep cures'.[63]

Today, doctors can prescribe numerous antidepressants and anxiolytics, and some people feel they benefit. However, the extent of the improvement attributable to the medicine remains, as we will see, controversial. While antidepressants have become gradually safer since the first modern medicines for depression emerged in the 1950s, their efficacy has not markedly improved. And modern antidepressants and anxiolytics can still cause serious side effects and withdrawal symptoms.

You need to carefully consider the risks and benefits of antidepressants and anxiolytics, and understand why a particular drug is right for you. However, discussing the evidence supporting the numerous antidepressants and anxiolytics and the equally valid criticisms would take a whole book. So, this chapter briefly outlines the main issues and the most widely used treatments to help you have an informed discussion.

Even drugs' most ardent supporters do not claim that antidepressants and anxiolytics cure depression or anxiety in the way that, for example, antibiotics cure bacterial infections. However, antidepressants and anxiolytics may alleviate symptoms, offering you the opportunity to address the causes. Indeed, lifestyle changes and psychotherapy seem to be as effective as antidepressants (and some antidepressants are also anxiolytics) for mild to moderate depression and anxiety. NICE, for instance, suggests offering people with persistent subthreshold symptoms or mild to moderate depression non-drug (psychological) treatments, such as cognitive behavioural therapy or group physical activity. Drugs might be appropriate if, for example, subthreshold or mild symptoms persist despite non-drug treatments, the person has previously experienced moderate or severe depression or has had subthreshold symptoms for a long time (for example, at least two years) before seeking medical help. People with moderate or severe depression should, NICE suggests, receive an antidepressant and a psychological treatment.

Biased studies: a word of caution

Developing a new medicine costs up to $1.3 billion.[64, 65] Not surprisingly, pharmaceutical companies design studies to give their drug the best chance of clinical and commercial success, while limiting the risk to vulnerable people. For example, clinical studies of antidepressants often exclude people at high risk of suicide.[44] Ironically, of course, these are also the people most likely to need help. In other words, many studies sponsored by manufacturers are biased. For instance, studies of medicines and medical devices sponsored by manufacturers are 31 per cent more likely to reach favourable conclusions, 32 per cent more likely to report favourable efficacy and 87 per cent more likely to report a favourable side effect profile than those funded in other ways.[66]

In addition, many negative studies are not published in medical journals. Researchers looked at 74 studies of antidepressants that pharmaceutical companies submitted to the Food and Drug Administration (FDA), which regulates medicines in the USA. They found that 37 of the 38 studies (98 per cent) with results favouring the antidepressant were published. Just three studies of the 38 – about 8 per cent – with unfavourable results were published. Another 11 'unsupportive' studies were reported in a way that, the authors believed, 'conveyed a positive outcome'. Most of the unfavourable studies were not published.[67] So, if healthcare professionals or patients looked only at the published literature, they would gain the impression that 94 per cent of studies supported antidepressants. When the researchers included the negative studies this fell to 51 per cent.[67] The study could not ascertain whether the authors did not submit negative studies, or the journal did not publish them (scientific journals tend to publish positive papers), or both.[67]

Whatever the cause, this selective publishing – which applies to many drugs – makes it difficult for doctors, nurses and patients to gain an accurate impression of the risks and benefits. It's usually better to rely on reviews by the Cochrane Collaboration (<www.cochrane.org>) or NICE (<www.nice.org.uk>). While these reviews lag behind the most recent data, they are not subject to commercial pressures, they include unpublished studies and publish summaries for patients to help you make informed decisions.

A warning

Never stop taking any antidepressant or anxiolytic, increase or decrease the dose or add another medicine – even bought without a prescription – without speaking to your doctor or pharmacist first.

- Antidepressants and anxiolytics can cause serious side effects. Increasing the dose is potentially dangerous.
- Coming off antidepressants and some anxiolytics can cause unpleasant and serious withdrawal reactions (page 44), which may resemble anxiety or depression.
- Several drugs, herbs (page 115) and even certain foods (page 39) can interact with antidepressants and anxiolytics triggering serious side effects.

So, follow your doctor's advice carefully, ask your pharmacist or doctor if you are uncertain and, if the professionals agree that it is safe to cut down, take your time and reduce the dose gradually.

Understanding antidepressants and anxiolytics

The brain and nervous system

Your brain makes the most powerful super-computer look like an especially simple pocket calculator. A computer cannot yet create the next *Mona Lisa*, write the next *Ulysses*, or compose the next hit single, let alone the next Bach concerto. This soft blob – writers compare its consistency to a jelly, soft tofu or warm butter – is responsible for your intelligence, emotions, personality, the way you interpret your environment and circumstances, and, in turn, your risk of developing depression and anxiety.

Your brain weighs just 1.3–1.4 kilograms (2.9–3.0 pounds), but contains about 100 billion cells. Each nerve cell (neurone) connects with many others, across 'gaps' called synapses, forming vast networks and 'pathways'. If you cut a brain open, areas dense in neurones look grey – they are literally your grey matter. Nerves connect every part of your body to your brain. The longest nerves run for an average of a metre from the base of the spine to the toes.[68] The trochlear nerve in the eye is, on average, just 86 mm long.[69] These connections mean that your brain knows almost immediately when you stub your big toe, touch a hot pan or hit your thumb with a hammer. The brain also passes signals to your body along these nerves to ensure your body meets the demands of the environment, such as increasing heartbeat, respiration and sweating as part of the fight-or-flight response.

A cocktail of chemical messengers

Neurones release chemical messengers that influence the activity of one or more additional nerves, muscles and organ cells. The integrated action of millions of neurones in the brain and the rest of the body allows us to think, move and live. Some nerves that run to and from the brain release chemical messengers, called neurotransmitters, that, for example, control heart rate, breathing and muscle tension. Many medicines act by mimicking or blocking the 100 or so of these neurotransmitters.

When the neurotransmitter reaches the next nerve, muscle or organ cell, it binds to a receptor. This transmits the signal. Imagine the nerve or muscle cell as a car. The receptor is the ignition. The neurotransmitter is the key. When the key fits into the ignition lock, the engine starts. Likewise, when the neurotransmitter binds to its receptor, part of the cell's internal machinery switches on increasing heart rate, muscle tension, sweat production and so on. This effect is specific: just as your key only starts your car, the messenger only switches on those processes controlled by the receptor.

Leaving your engine running at full revs would damage your car and burn off too much petrol. Over-stimulating cells can damage the body and use food we might need when there is less around. (Our ancestors couldn't just pop to the supermarket or take-away.) So, the body evolved several ways to curtail the neurotransmitter's action. For example, an enzyme called monoamine oxidase (MAO) breaks down four chemical messengers: dopamine, adrenaline, noradrenaline and serotonin. For example, serotonin seems to regulate several bodily functions, including sleep, eating and mood.[176] As we've seen, these functions often go awry in depression. Noradrenaline seems to be involved in our reactions to stress, alertness, energy and interest in life. Dopamine may contribute to motivation, pleasure and 'reward-seeking' behaviours.[176] As a we've also seen, a lack of interest in activities and events that were previously pleasurable is one of the most important hallmarks of depression. A group of antidepressants called MAO inhibitors (MAOI) block MAO, allowing levels of the neurotransmitters to rise and continue to stimulate the receptors.

Some nerves take the neurotransmitters back into the terminal before the synapse. This 'recycles' the neurotransmitter. Blocking this 'reuptake' increases levels of neurotransmitter in the synapse. Tricyclic antidepressants (TCAs) inhibit the reuptake of noradrenaline, serotonin and, to a lesser extent, dopamine.[70] As their name suggests, selective serotonin reuptake inhibitors (SSRIs) boost levels of serotonin.

Now imagine that you have a skeleton key that fits the ignition lock and switches on the engine. Some drugs act like a skeleton key. The receptor cannot distinguish the drug from the neurotransmitter. Both switch on the cell's machinery. Other drugs fit the receptor, preventing the usual messenger from reaching the receptor. However, the drug does not switch on the cell's machinery. These drugs are 'antagonists' or 'blockers'. Doctors may treat certain symptoms caused by anxiety with beta blockers (page 52). These block adrenaline and noradrenaline from reaching their receptors. So, beta blockers reduce heart rate and blood pressure.

Cheese and dancing TB patients

Doctors discovered the first modern antidepressants by accident. During the late 1950s, researchers were testing a drug called iproniazid for tuberculosis. To their surprise, people with tuberculosis taking iproniazid showed 'striking' psychological changes, in particular, more vitality. Iproniazid even produced a party mood and dancing among people critically ill with tuberculosis. Doctors soon found that iproniazid, the first MAOI, enhanced mood in people with other chronic illnesses, including rheumatoid arthritis, cancer and depression.[63] Other MAOIs – including isocarboxazid, tranylcypromine and phenelzine – followed.[63] But they had an Achilles' heel: the 'cheese effect'.

Cheese and several other foods – including yeast products, liver, snails, pickled herrings, red wines, some beers, tinned figs, broad beans, fermented soya bean products, and chocolate – contain high levels of an amino acid (the building blocks of protein) called tyramine. MAO breaks down tyramine. So, levels of tyramine rise in people taking MAOIs. In some people, high levels of tyramine provoked dangerous increases in blood pressure.[63] Swedish cheddar eventually emerged as the 'most dangerous cheese' when taken with MAOIs.[71]

More recently developed MAOIs alleviate depression, but leave enough of the enzyme to break down usual levels of tyramine, which means diet is not as much of an issue.[8] However, some people are especially sensitive to tyramine. So, avoid large amounts of tyramine when you take MAOIs. Speak to your doctor or pharmacist and make sure you fully understand the dietary restrictions.

Tricyclic antidepressants

Another group of antidepressants – the TCAs – trace their origins to the search for a treatment for schizophrenia. In the 1950s, clinicians found that one drug, called imipramine, did not control all the effects of schizophrenia. However, people taking imipramine voluntarily got up, spoke less quietly and more fluently, showed more lively facial expressions, made more contact with other people, played games and laughed.[63] Imipramine soon became a popular antidepressant and other TCAs followed, including amitriptyline, desipramine and nortriptyline. Although TCAs do not cause the cheese effect, they can cause a variety of unpleasant side effects including:[63, 70]

- blurred vision
- constipation
- disorientation
- dizziness
- memory disorders
- poor hand–eye coordination
- sedation
- orthostatic (postural) hypotension: low blood pressure on standing up, which can cause fainting
- urine retention
- serious cardiovascular side effects (which affect the heart and blood vessels).

Because of the cardiovascular side effects, TCAs can prove fatal in overdose. To make matters worse, the safety margin is a very low,[70] making deliberate or accidental overdose easy. More recently, studies linked TCAs and several other drugs – such as some hay fever treatments and certain medicines for bladder problems – to an increased likelihood of developing Alzheimer's disease. All these drugs block a neurotransmitter called acetylcholine – an effect that contributes to TCAs' adverse events. People with Alzheimer's disease also show reduced levels of acetylcholine, which seems to be important in memory, attention and other elements of cognition ('thinking').[72]

Overall, between 27 and 60 per cent of people taking TCAs stop treatment, usually following side effects. Meanwhile, concerns about

Risks and benefits

The decision to take any medicine means balancing risks and benefits. Even everyday medicines can cause serious side effects; for instance, paracetamol can damage the liver, while aspirin can cause bleeding in the gut. Even psychotherapies (page 57) and spirituality (page 101) carry certain risks. So, discuss your choice of drug fully with your doctor, read the package insert and check out other sources of information, such as NHS Choices (<www.nhs.uk>) and the electronic Medicines Compendium (<www.medicines.org.uk>).

side effects led many GPs to prescribe too low a dose to be effective as an antidepressant. The search was on for a safer antidepressant.

Towards the Prozac nation

Prozac is one of the few drug brand names – along with aspirin, heroin and Viagra – to have entered the general language. All drugs have a scientific name and one or more brand names. Prozac is the brand name for fluoxetine, which is an SSRI. (For the record, the scientific names for aspirin, heroin and Viagra are acetylsalicylic acid, diacetylmorphine and sildenafil respectively.) Other SSRIs include paroxetine, sertraline and fluvoxamine.

Unlike MAOIs and TCAs, which researchers discovered by accident, pharmaceutical companies specifically designed SSRIs to tackle depression. As we have seen, TCAs and MAOIs increase levels of serotonin (also called 5-hydroxytryptamine, abbreviated as 5HT) and other neurotransmitters. So, pharmaceutical companies designed SSRIs to increase 5HT levels by selectively blocking a protein called the 'serotonin reuptake transporter'. This 'pump' transports 5HT back into the nerve before the synapse. Blocking the pump 'tricks' the nerve into believing serotonin levels in the synapse are low. So, the nerve releases more serotonin.[70,73] Blocking the pump also keeps more transmitter in the synapse.

A more recently developed group of drugs – which includes venlafaxine and duloxetine – blocks reuptake of serotonin and noradrenaline. Some people find these serotonin–noradrenaline reuptake inhibitors (SNRIs) work when SSRIs fail. Another drug called reboxetine strongly inhibits noradrenaline reuptake, but only weakly influences serotonin reuptake.[74]

SSRIs' side effects

NICE points out that TCAs, MAOIs and SSRIs show broadly similar efficacy. So, doctors choose antidepressants based on other factors, including side effects, your preference, whether you have any other ailments and the risk of withdrawal symptoms. SSRIs produce fewer cardiovascular effects than TCAs and are relatively safe if taken in over-dose.[63] Nevertheless, SSRIs can cause numerous side effects including:[63]

- diarrhoea
- drowsiness
- dry mouth
- insomnia

The tianeptine enigma

As we have seen, most antidepressants increase the amount of serotonin in the synapse by reducing reuptake (SSRIs and TCAs) or inhibiting breakdown (MAOIs). However, an antidepressant called tianeptine *increases* the amount of serotonin taken up by the nerve and so *reduces* the amount in the synapse. Yet tianeptine, which isn't approved in the UK, alleviates depression and anxiety.[74] Tianeptine's paradoxical action is not the only factor that calls the link between neurotransmitters and depression into question. For instance, the brain rapidly compensates for the increased serotonin levels in people taking SSRIs.[75] Furthermore, TCAs alleviate several anxiety disorders, from panic disorder to OCD.[44] SSRIs are approved for numerous psychiatric conditions including depression, social anxiety, premenstrual tension (which psychiatrists call premenstrual dysphoric disorder) and OCD. Biologists haven't convincingly explained how an abnormality in a single neurotransmitter 'could result in so many widely differing behavioural manifestations'. Such observations suggest that changes in neurotransmitters probably do not directly cause depression and anxiety.[75] Furthermore, if low levels of the transmitters caused anxiety and depression, it is difficult to explain why drugs that increase transmitter levels typically take several weeks to improve the symptoms of depression. Such observations suggest that antidepressants work indirectly.[182] The observations also show that we are a long way from understanding either the link between these neurotransmitters and anxiety and depression, or how antidepressants work.

- long-term weight gain
- nausea
- nervousness
- sexual problems
- short-term weight loss
- skin reactions
- sweating.

Furthermore, almost half of people who responded to antidepressants would not take them again because of psychological side effects including:[44]

- inability to cry;
- loss of creativity;
- not feeling like oneself;
- reduced emotional range, the so-called narrowing of affect – you may feel fewer downs, but you also cannot feel peaks of happiness.

In addition, SSRIs and some other antidepressants can cause sexual side effects, such as decreased libido, delayed or pleasureless orgasm, inability to have an orgasm, and reduced arousal. In the clinical studies, between 2 and 16 per cent of people taking antidepressants reported sexual side effects. Other studies suggest the figure is much higher: 62 per cent in men and 57 per cent in women.[44] So, swallow your embarrassment and speak to your GP if you think that your antidepressant or another medicine is causing sexual side effects.

The SSRI–suicide link

Severe depression increases the risk of suicide (page 19). So, you might expect antidepressants to prevent self-harm – and some studies suggest that this is the case.[76] Yet in some circumstances, for some patients, SSRIs may make suicide *more* likely. For example, antidepressants often improve energy and motivation before mood starts to lift. You can remain suicidal, but now have the energy and drive to self-harm. Young people seem to be at especially high risk.

- The FDA reviewed 24 studies involving 4,400 people. About 1 in 25 young people taking antidepressants reported suicidal behaviour or thoughts, twice the rate among those taking a placebo, despite similar levels of depression.[44]

- Other studies suggest that SSRIs double the risk that a person with depression will attempt suicide compared to taking a placebo. However, it's important to keep these risks in perspective. On average, one additional suicide attempt occurs every 179 years of SSRI use.[77]
- Researchers enrolled 162,625 people in the USA aged 10 to 64 years who started SSRIs. The rate of deliberate self-harm among people 24 years of age or younger beginning high-dose SSRIs was approximately twice that among similar people starting the average dose. Overall, about one person self-harmed for every 136 people aged 10 to 24 years starting high-dose SSRIs.[78]

So, it's important to watch for suicide's warning signs (page 21) when you or a relative starts antidepressants. Doctors should see people at increased risk of suicide – including those aged less than 30 years – a week after starting antidepressants, NICE suggests. GPs should also see those at increased risk more frequently than other people with depression.

Withdrawal symptoms

Not stopping or reducing the dose without speaking to your GP first is especially important if you are taking antidepressants: withdrawal (also called discontinuation) symptoms can occur when you stop treatment, or miss or reduce the dose (Table 3.1). Doctors typically suggest that withdrawal symptoms are mild, emerge 1 or 2 days after stopping and resolve after 1 or 2 weeks. However, some people experience severe withdrawal symptoms, particularly after suddenly stopping.

Nevertheless, an online survey study of 1829 people in New Zealand found that 55 per cent experienced withdrawal effects after stopping antidepressants. Indeed, 43 per cent endured 'moderate' or 'severe' symptoms. Moreover, 27 per cent felt that they were addicted to antidepressants, with 16 per cent experiencing 'moderate' or 'severe' addiction. Addiction and withdrawal effects seemed to be intertwined. For instance, 87 per cent of those reporting addiction also experienced withdrawal effects.[202]

The general public's use of the words 'addiction' and 'withdrawal symptoms' may not be the same as the definitions used by researchers or clinicians (although the authors point out that experts' definitions of addiction 'vary considerably'). Nevertheless, it's clear that many people experience difficulties when they try to stop or reduce their antidepressants.[202]

When you agree with your doctor that the time is right, you will reduce the dose of your antidepressant over at least four weeks – often longer for some drugs (such as paroxetine or venlafaxine). If you

Table 3.1 Withdrawal symptoms with antidepressants

Antidepressant	Common symptoms	Occasional symptoms
MAOIs	Agitation Ataxia (problems with coordination, balance and speech) Cognitive impairment (e.g. problems with mental abilities such as thinking, knowing and remembering) Insomnia Irritability Movement disorders Rapid, frenzied, pressured speech Slowed speech Somnolence (excessive sleepiness) Vivid dreams	Hallucinations Paranoid delusions
TCAs	Diarrhoea Flu-like symptoms Headache Insomnia Lethargy Nausea and vomiting Restlessness Vivid and increased dreaming	Cardiac arrhythmias (abnormal heartbeat) Mania Movement disorders
SSRIs/Venlafaxine	Abdominal cramps Agitation Crying spells Dizziness Electric shock sensations in the head Fatigue Flu-like symptoms Insomnia Irritability Sensory disturbance Vertigo Vivid and increased dreaming	Movement disorders Poor concentration Poor memory

Source Adapted from NHS Scotland: <www.nes.scot.NHS.UK/media/344033/stoppingantide pressants.pdf>

develop severe withdrawal symptoms, the doctor may restart a higher dose and reduce even more gradually.

How effective are antidepressants?

A surgeon operating near the front line during the Korean War began suffering severe abdominal pain, which he knew indicated acute appendicitis. As incoming wounded needed his help, he asked the nurse to give him an injection of morphine. The pain eased and he kept working. With the crisis over, the doctor underwent surgery to remove his appendix.[79]

After returning to duty, the doctor was looking through the operating room records and found that 'since he appeared distressed' the nurse had injected inactive saline and not morphine.[79] (She probably wanted to avoid the mental fogging that morphine can cause.)

In other words, a simple salt solution used to mix injectable drugs alleviated the severe pain of acute appendicitis. Critically, however, the surgeon *expected* the nurse to follow his instructions. He *expected* to receive morphine. This expectation invoked the placebo effect – his mind and body reacted as if he had received the morphine. For example, placebos can increase levels of the body's natural painkillers and counter anxiety, which heightens sensitivity to pain.

The placebo effect

The 'placebo response' – the term derives from the Latin for 'I shall please' – contributes to the effectiveness of every drug you take, every complementary treatment or psychotherapy you try, every lifestyle change you make. Here are some examples.

- People with irritable bowel syndrome (IBS) experience stomach cramps and pain, bloating, diarrhoea and constipation. On average, placebo responses account for around 40 per cent of the benefit of an IBS treatment. However, depending on the study, the placebo response in IBS can vary between 16 and 71 per cent.[80]
- Two hours after taking soluble aspirin, 27 per cent of migraine sufferers were pain-free, compared to 33 per cent taking ibuprofen and 37 per cent with sumatriptan (a medicine taken specifically for migraine). The placebo response was 13 per cent.[81]
- In psoriasis – where an abnormal immune reaction targets the skin and sometimes joints – the placebo response is between 5 and 30 per cent.[82]

Several factors contribute to the placebo effect, including the ones listed below.

- The brain may release painkillers and other 'feel good' chemicals after we take a drug we expect to work.
- We expect doctors to help. Doctors who raise our expectations and optimism, who are enthusiastic about the treatment, who are confident, authoritative, empathic, charismatic and warm seem to bolster the placebo effect.[19, 79]
- Going to a doctor and receiving a treatment relieves anxiety, while placebos evoke positive, optimistic thoughts, which help counter depression.[79] Placebos, Irving Kirsch notes, 'instil hope . . . by promising [people with depression] relief from their distress'.[6]
- Some people's desire to believe, 'obey' and please the doctor tends to enhance the placebo response.[19]
- Time is a great healer. Up to 90 per cent of acute (short-lived) diseases improve regardless of treatment.[18] A flare of arthritis can abate. Anxiety passes. A low mood improves – as we have seen, often without a major change to a person's lifestyle or circumstances. Over time, these ebbs and flows average out. But many people attribute this natural improvement to the medicine or treatment.

The placebo response and depression

In some studies antidepressants produce an especially marked placebo response, which may account for up to 82 per cent of their benefit.[44]

More recent research seems to suggest, however, that antidepressants produce a 'modest' improvement in symptoms. Researchers examined 522 studies including 87,052 people who received antidepressants and 29,425 taking an inactive placebo. It was found that about 90 per cent of patients had moderate to severe depression.[208]

All the 21 antidepressants studied were more effective than the placebo, based on the proportion of people who showed at least a 50 per cent reduction in symptom score. Amitriptyline, mirtazapine, duloxetine, venlafaxine and paroxetine emerged as the five most effective antidepressants. Treatment acceptability – the proportion discontinuing for any reason (including lack of efficacy and side effects) – was, for most drugs, no different from the placebo. Agomelatine and fluoxetine, however, were associated with fewer dropouts than the placebo. Clomipramine was worse than the placebo. The analysis, however, examined only average effects and not factors that may influence an individual's

When placebos harm

Over the years, we have become better informed about medicines. We recognize that there is no pharmacological free lunch. Just as we expect a benefit from a medicine, we expect side effects. And just as placebos can improve symptoms, they can cause side effects.[83] Doctors call this the 'nocebo' effect – from the Latin for 'I shall harm'. For example, people who received TCA placebos were around three times more likely to report dry mouth, drowsiness and constipation, and about twice as likely to report sexual problems as those on SSRI placebos. All these side effects are more common with TCAs than SSRIs.[84]

response to treatment, such as age, sex, severity of symptom or duration of illness. In addition, the analysis focused on outcomes at eight weeks, whereas most people need long-term treatment.[208] Nevertheless, while people need to be able to choose the approach to treatment that's right for them, the new study confirms that some people benefit from antidepressants.

To complicate matters further, most studies use depression rating scales to assess antidepressants' effectiveness. The rating scales include some symptoms that are not specific to depression, such as sleeping problems, anxiety, agitation and physical ailments. Many of these respond to antidepressants' non-specific effects (in other words, effects other than those directly targeting mood). Most TCAs and SSRIs are strong and mild sedatives respectively, for example. In addition, drugs such as benzodiazepines and opiates seem to work in people with depression, partly by reducing anxiety and agitation.[35] As we have seen, antidepressants also reduce emotional sensitivity.

In other words, antidepressants may sometimes produce non-specific effects rather than targeting depression. The non-specific benefits and side effects mean that you can guess whether you received a placebo or active medicine. Knowing that you have taken an active medicine seems to boost the placebo effect.

In addition, most people need to take antidepressants for several weeks, or even months, before the hopelessness, helplessness and suicidal thoughts abate.[33] Improved sleeping, more regular eating, a sense of calm and more energy are often the first benefits. Mood begins to lift after four weeks or so.[15] Be careful, especially at first, about tasks that require alertness and coordination, such as driving or operating heavy machinery. For the first few weeks at least, it is prudent to avoid

Residual symptoms

Around 30 to 50 per cent of people endure residual symptoms between bouts of major depression including low energy, guilt, sleep disturbance, anxiety, difficulties at work, lack of interest, fatigue and low libido. They might also experience somatic symptoms (page 8) such as low back pain, muscle pain and stomach ache.[86]

alcohol, which further undermines alertness and coordination. Always ask your doctor how much alcohol it is safe to drink when taking an antidepressant or anxiolytic.

You will need to stay on treatment for several months. NICE suggests continuing antidepressants for at least 6 months after the remission of an episode of depression. People at high risk of relapse – for example, because they have at least two recent debilitating bouts of depression or because they have residual symptoms[85] – should continue antidepressants for at least 2 years. Between 40 and 50 per cent of people with major depression relapse if they stop taking antidepressants. Continuing treatment reduces the proportion of patients who relapse to between 13 and 20 per cent.[85]

Nevertheless, around 30 per cent of people with depression do not respond adequately to current antidepressants.[63] You might want to discuss a switch to a different drug, such as one with a noradrenergic element may help if a SSRI fails to produce an adequate improvement.

Other treatments for depression

The limitations of existing drugs led to doctors investigating other drug treatments for depression, to improve efficacy and reduce side effects.

- Ketamine, which is an anaesthetic and a street drug, improves severe depression that does not respond to other antidepressants. Ketamine's antidepressant effects can emerge within two hours of the injection and a single treatment's effects last for between three and ten days.[33, 34] Ketamine can cause side effects, including changes in vital signs, blurred vision, drowsiness and sleepiness, and psychotic, manic and dissociative symptoms. Nevertheless, studies into ketamine raise the prospect of new antidepressants for people who do not respond to conventional drugs.[87] Indeed, *Science*, a leading journal, described ketamine's benefits as 'arguably the most important discovery [in depression] in half a century'.[34]

- Antipsychotics are usually prescribed for very severe mental illnesses, such as schizophrenia or bipolar disorder. However, antipsychotics are also used for anxiety, depression, sleep disorders, OCD and PTSD. The dose tends to be lower and duration of treatment shorter than for schizophrenia. However, antipsychotics can cause serious side effects including: movement disorders – including spasms, an unpleasant feeling of restlessness, irregular jerks as well as symptoms similar to Parkinson's disease; weight gain; and, in some people, heart disease and strokes.[88]
- Electroconvulsive therapy (ECT) might be an option if people are: severely suicidal; neglect their heath or personal hygiene, health and so on; have psychotic depression (page 3); or cannot take medicines. The doctor gives the person a light anaesthetic and a drug that relaxes their muscles. The electric current then passes through the brain for a split second. Typically, a doctor might suggest between 6 and 12 ECT treatments. Patients may experience loss of memory of events just before the ECT and for two or weeks afterwards. Some people also experience nausea, confusion or headaches and aching muscles. Doctors do not fully understand how ECT works. But, perhaps not surprisingly, ECT seems to affect every neurotransmitter.
- Transcranial magnetic stimulation (TMS) uses magnetic fields to stimulate nerve cells in the region of your brain involved in mood control and depression. Studies indicate that TMS is only slightly more effective than a placebo. However, TMS may be effective for treatment-resistant depression. NICE comments that currently there seem to be 'no major safety concerns'. Nevertheless, TMS might trigger seizures or mania, or result in local scalp discomfort, headache, nausea, neck stiffness and hearing loss.

Speak to your doctor if you want to discuss these approaches and always make sure you understand the risks and benefits.

Anxiolytics

Over the centuries, people tried countless drugs to alleviate anxiety, including cannabis, alcohol, betel nuts, opium, nicotine and barbiturates (such as phenobarbital). However, the introduction of meprobamate (branded as Miltown and Equanil) in the 1950s, followed by the benzodiazepines chlordiazepoxide (Librium) and diazepam (Valium) in the 1960s and early 1970s, added anxiety to the list of conditions that doctors and patients thought medicines could treat.[59] Indeed, drug companies promoted tranquillizers for a wide range of life's problems and difficulties, including tension, nerves, the menopause, and family, marital and work difficulties. The market was massive: 1 in 20 Americans had used meprobamate within a year of its introduction.[59]

Today psychotherapy, rather than medicines, is the treatment of choice, and the two approaches show broadly similar short-term benefits in anxiety.[49] However, as mentioned before, drugs do not tackle the underlying problems that cause anxiety. Indeed, drugs are rarely used to treat certain anxiety disorders, such as specific phobias, illness anxiety or separation anxiety disorder.[49] Nevertheless, anxiolytics remain useful and can provide immediate relief (e.g. benzodiazepines) or longer-lasting remission (e.g. SSRIs).[49] For instance, anxiolytics can help while you are waiting for psychotherapy,[49] if you experience symptoms during psychotherapy or you are having a particularly bad time.

NICE suggests that SSRIs are the first-line medicine for GAD or panic disorder. If the SSRI has not adequately alleviated symptoms after, for example, four weeks, your doctor may suggest another anxiolytic such as pregabalin or venlafaxine.[49] If you show some improvement with the SSRI after four weeks, you should discuss continuing as the benefit often increases.[89] As a rough guide, one in every five people taking drugs for GAD and PTSD benefit.[49] This means that four-fifths of those taking drugs respectively do not benefit, but may still experience side effects.

SSRIs are the most widely used drugs for anxiety disorders, PTSD and OCD. The choice between individual SSRIs depends on, for example, side effects, interactions, ease of discontinuation and so on.[49] Some people find that their GAD, PTSD and panic disorder worsen for the first few weeks after starting an SSRI, TCA or other antidepressant.[49] So, doctors tend to start with a lower dose than used in depression and monitor efficacy and side effects regularly, such as every two to four weeks for the first three months. To reduce the risk that your anxiety will recur, take the antidepressant for at least:

- 6 months after symptoms of panic disorder and social anxiety disorder improve;
- 12 months after symptoms of PTSD and OCD improve;
- up to 18 months after GAD symptoms improve.[49]

Tranquillizers

A minor tranquillizer reduces anxiety for between four and six hours. A sedative is stronger and causes sleep.[15] (Our sleep hygiene tips on page 120 should help you get a good night's rest without medicines.) Benzodiazepines rapidly relieve severe or disabling attacks of GAD, social anxiety and panic disorder that cause unacceptable distress. However, benzodiazepines do not seem to be effective in OCD.[49]

Classic tranquillizers, such as the benzodiazepines, are very addictive and can cause withdrawal symptoms, including flu-like complaints, muscle cramps, irritability, insomnia, nightmares, perceptual changes, depersonalization or derealization. Benzodiazepines' withdrawal symptoms can be difficult to distinguish from anxiety.[90] Indeed, some people report worse panic attacks after stopping benzodiazepines.[49] Used long-term, benzodiazepines can increase the risk of road traffic accidents, dependence, tolerance and falls.[49] So, benzodiazepines should be used for two to four weeks only.[49] Withdrawal from long-term benzodiazepines must be gradual.[49]

Other treatments for anxiety

Other treatments for anxiety disorders include the following.

- Beta blockers, also known as beta-adrenoceptor blocking agents (e.g. propranolol and oxprenolol; page 39), can alleviate physical symptoms of anxiety, such as palpitations, tremor, sweating and shortness of breath. Beta blockers are especially useful when a particular circumstance, such as giving a presentation, triggers the anxiety. People with anxiety often report dizziness or postural hypotension, which beta blockers can exacerbate.[49] Postural (also called orthostatic) hypotension refers to low blood pressure when you stand up. The low blood pressure can leave you feeling dizzy or lightheaded and maybe even faint.
- Pregabalin often alleviates acute GAD within a few days and seems to reduce the risk of relapses. A doctor may suggest pregabalin for GAD if antidepressants cause unacceptable side effects. Pregabalin's side effects include dizziness and somnolence (sleepiness or drowsiness).[49]
- Buspirone is effective in GAD and does not cause sedation, withdrawal symptoms or dependence.[89] Buspirone's side effects include dizziness, headache, nervousness, light-headedness, nausea, excitement, sleepiness, and sweating or clamminess.
- Between 10 per cent and 20 per cent of people with OCD do not respond adequately to drugs and CBT. A few people with severe

persistent OCD may be suitable for surgery that cuts the network of nerves that seem to generate OCD. Between 45 per cent and 70 per cent with treatment-resistant, severe OCD who undergo this operation – called cingulotomy – show a long-term improvement.[91]

Between 14 per cent and 43 per cent of people with anxiety disorders do not respond to medicines or CBT. Another 18 per cent to 48 per cent relapse within 6 months.[3] This may mean that you need a different psychotherapy, need to change your lifestyle, or both.

4

Talking therapies: beyond the couch

Cognitive behavioural therapy (CBT) and the other psychotherapies (talking therapies) are usually the treatment of choice for depression or anxiety. Increasingly, doctors prescribe antidepressants and anxiolytics only for severe depression or anxiety, often combined with psychotherapy, or when non-drug treatments do not offer sufficient relief.

As we have seen, antidepressants and anxiolytics paper over your psychological cracks. Psychotherapy, in contrast, can help you understand the causes of your anxiety and depression, and implement changes to make your life easier. For instance, unresolved sadness can lead to depression, exaggerated fear to anxiety, and anger to hostility and resentment (see Table 4.1). This, in turn, can create a variety of abnormal behaviours.[92] Psychotherapy can also help you deal with your counterproductive behaviours. However, there are more than 500 psychotherapies[93] and you need to find the right approach for you.

The thought trap

Many people with depression and anxiety become trapped in cycles of damaging, counterproductive thoughts. A person with anxiety may generalize from a single event to seeing threats everywhere. Many people with anxiety ruminate about a future event, imagining dire consequences. Depressed people feel intensely guilty that they did not do something different – even if there was nothing that they realistically could have done.

In particular, people with depression and anxiety tend to overestimate the likelihood that a problem will arise and the chances that the difficulty will prove catastrophic. After all, as Tallis notes in *How To Stop Worrying* (see Futher reading), if you've had a run of bad luck 'it will be difficult for you to maintain a positive picture of the world'. At least pessimism helps you prepare. If you imagine the worst, then you can be relieved that the outcome is not as bad as you expected. But expecting bad news can easily become a self-fulfilling prophecy.

Living with depression and anxiety is intensely stressful. So, people may use 'coping strategies' to alleviate their distress by 'distorting'

Table 4.1 Signs of problems caused by withholding emotions

Physical signs

Bruxism (teeth grinding)
Headaches
Hypertension (dangerously raised blood pressure)
Indigestion and other gastrointestinal problems
Muscle tension
Physical fatigue (e.g. weakness or lack of strength)
Reduced resistance to infections, such as colds and reactivation of cold sores

Emotional signs

Boredom
Emotionally drained or 'burnt out'
Helplessness
Irritability
Lethargy
Withdrawal

Mental (psychological) signs

Errors (e.g. at work or when dealing with household finances)
Forgetfulness
Insomnia or excessive sleep
Pessimism
Pickiness
Poor concentration
'Tunnel vision' (focusing on one issue and neglecting or ignoring other important concerns)

Source Adapted from Dugan[92]

reality or altering their self-perception. These 'coping strategies' can tide you over a rough patch and allow you to tackle immediate problems. However, at best these are short-term fixes. Allowing an adverse coping strategy to become entrenched can leave you unable to deal with your underlying problems.

Repression and denial

Repression is one of the most powerful – and one of the most dangerous – adverse coping strategies: we banish unpleasant thoughts or guilty memories from our conscious minds. We might, for example, repress memories of maltreatment, or being lonely or bullied as a child. However, these lurk in the subconscious and can re-emerge – sometimes as a flashback, sometimes in a distorted, almost unrecognizable form (perhaps as an obsession or phobia, for example) – triggering stress, depression and anxiety and undermining our ability to cope. Psychoanalysts may need to uncover repressed memories to resolve the stress, anxiety and depression. Not surprisingly, this can, at first, prove distressing.

Denial focuses on current (rather than past) events and allows us to avoid accepting the reality of our situation – even when we face overwhelming evidence. Drug addicts, gamblers and alcoholics typically minimize or deny the harm that they do to themselves and others. Alcoholics Anonymous and other rehabilitation programmes succeed partly because they help people to face their addictions and the consequences.

Aggression and anger

Anger can be a valuable safety valve. However, anger can frighten people around you, may lead to legal complications if aggression gets out of hand, and trigger serious illness. For example, one study found that the risk of a stroke was almost eight-fold higher in the two hours after an angry outburst. Anger also drives blood pressure up. So, an aneurysm (a weak area of a blood vessel) is about six times more likely to burst in the two hours after an angry outburst,[94] which can cause a stroke or heart attack. Try to accept your anger and channel your aggression and other emotions more productively. Talking to a counsellor or therapist may help you understand why you react with anger when facing problems and help you develop a better coping mechanism.

Withdrawal and procrastination

Retreating into a mental shell can be a sensible 'strategic withdrawal', offering people the time and space to re-evaluate their lives, priorities and problems. However, some people narrow their horizons until their lives are within limits they think they can control, which may be very limited. Taken to extremes, withdrawal encourages apathy, depression and isolation from friends, family, work and other social networks. Some people who withdraw from social interactions feel that they lack confidence: assertiveness training and interpersonal therapy might make life a little easier.

Procrastination can also alleviate stress and anxiety in the short term. However, over the long term procrastination increases stress[21] as problems and unfinished tasks build up. So, you need to develop effective ways to identify and tackle problems (page 66).

Talking therapies

Classic psychoanalysis

Psychotherapy can help you identify and change these counterproductive coping strategies. Classic psychoanalysis involves a Freud-like figure listening to you as you lie on a couch. As you relax and talk, unconscious thoughts rise to the surface, which the analyst helps you understand and come to terms with. Freudian analysis follows principles that Sigmund Freud laid down around a century ago, updated to the twenty-first century, and often provides profound insights into our nature, behaviours and motivations.

Freudian analysis is worth considering if you have the time and the money. You may need more than one session per week – sometimes four or five times a week – for several years. In addition, Freud transformed our understanding of the nature of behaviour, desires and motivations. So, many other therapists employ insights and elements of therapy pioneered by Freud. Contact the British Psychoanalytical Society or British Psychoanalytic Council.

Jungian approaches

Originally, the Swiss psychiatrist and psychotherapist Carl Jung followed Freud's approach. However, Jung felt that Freud did not place enough emphasis on the cultural, intellectual and spiritual dimensions of anxiety, depression and other mental problems. Jung, for example, suggested that anxiety, depression and other neuroses draw our attention to a side of our personality that we have neglected or repressed. This prevents the person from moving to their next stage in their personal development. Jungian analysis – called analytical psychoanalysis – helps us explore our neglected or repressed sides.

In addition to talking, Jungian therapy may include creative activities such as painting, drama, dance, playing with sand, writing a dream journal and listening to music. Indeed, while more studies are needed to characterize the benefits fully, music therapy plus usual treatment (such as drugs) may be more effective than usual treatment alone in people with depression. When researchers reviewed the evidence, they found that music therapy seems to reduce symptoms of depression and anxiety as well as improving people's ability to function in everyday life, such as at work and in their activities and relationships.[183]

Such self-expression can help you engage your inner creativity that is usually inhibited by societal, moral or ethical values. Understanding your self-imposed censors, and letting your creativity loose, can help you appreciate factors that may contribute to your depression and anxiety. Again, you may need to make a considerable commitment to analytical psychoanalysis. Contact the British Psychotherapy Foundation.

Freudian analysis and analytical psychoanalysis explore very deep layers of your personality to draw a detailed map of your subconscious, identify potential sources of trauma and conflict, and address the sources of your anxiety and depression. This deep excavation is one reason why Freudian and analytical psychoanalysis can take several years. After all, you may have a lifetime of experiences, conflicts and issues to work through. However, not everyone has the time and money to undergo 'full psychoanalysis'.

Behavioural therapies

Many newer psychotherapies take a 'behavioural approach' focusing on specific problems and symptoms rather than mounting a deep exploration of your underlying conflicts and issues. A behavioural therapist helps you clarify your problem, identify its impact on your life and those around you, and devise approaches to tackle the issues. While you still need to be committed, behavioural approaches are much more rapid than Freudian and analytical psychoanalysis. For example, group-based CBT for mild to moderate depression might consist of 10 to 12 meetings of 8 to 10 participants over 12 to 16 weeks. You can also have one-to-one CBT sessions, or use books and online courses (page 70).

Furthermore, Showalter comments in *Hystories: Hysterical epidemics and modern culture*,[20] 'softer, more approachable' figures have largely replaced the 'old-style authoritarian shrink'. Increasingly, a therapist is 'a comforting friend', who affirms and supports. Therapists have no preconceptions or agenda. They make no judgements about you. Unlike talking to family or friends, your choices do not affect the therapist's life, so his or her insights, combined with experience and training, mean that the therapist usually offers more objective and practical help than a friend can do.[15] Therapists don't replace your friends, of course. Both offer potentially helpful insights and suggestions from different perspectives.

Behavioural approaches can be effective, especially when delivered by a counsellor or therapist whom you trust. However, behavioural approaches have limitations. CBT, for example, is highly structured. So, CBT may not be suitable for people with more complex mental health needs. Furthermore, behavioural approaches focus on current problems and specific issues and symptoms. They do not allow you to explore and come to terms with the possible underlying causes of your depression and anxiety, such as an unhappy childhood. Indeed, classic Freudian analysts believe that focusing on behaviours can mean that the underlying distress will emerge in other dysfunctional ways. In addition, focusing on symptoms may mean you do not have the opportunity to grow emotionally and spiritually as you understand the personal significance, causes and meanings of your anxiety and depression.[47]

CBT and other behavioural approaches focus on the individual's capacity to change their thoughts, feelings and behaviours. They do not directly address wider problems, such as problems within families, that often influence health and well-being. You may decide to use CBT to tackle the immediate distressing issues and then invest in formal psychoanalysis to understand the deep-seated causes.

Choose the right therapist

Adverse coping strategies are, essentially, defences that protect our mental health. So, psychotherapy can prove distressing by, for example, uncovering memories you wish had stayed forgotten or drawing attention to sides of your personality and behaviour that you would rather remained in the shadows. Therapy can also create a narrative that tells the story of your suffering in a way that can be harrowing. In other words, psychotherapy involves confronting deeply held emotions, beliefs and anxieties. You may have to share some intimate thoughts with a stranger. So, you need to find a therapist that you are comfortable talking to, especially as you may experience periods where you are more anxious or emotionally uncomfortable.

Peter's story

Peter lived with numerous fragmented memories of childhood physical and emotional maltreatment and neglect by his mother and father, as well as severe bullying at school, which ended up to regular trips to the sick room and occasionally A&E and the GP. 'The events seemed like pieces of a jigsaw,' Peter said. 'An image or memory would pop up, but these didn't usually link together'. His psychotherapist placed the memories in order to help understand the chain of events that led to his depression and anxiety, his sporadic alcohol problem, and his inability to reach his potential at work or in relationships. Peter soon saw that the physical abuse, emotional neglect and bullying inside and outside the family lasted for longer and was more severe than he recalled – he'd repressed many of the most unpleasant memories. He also realized that no one in his family, school or health service intervened despite numerous opportunities. The insights made him more distressed, exacerbated his depression and deepened his resentment. He stopped going to the psychotherapist. He has benefited from CBT in his day-to-day life, but the insights still haunt him.

Cognitive behavioural therapy

In 1976, the American psychiatrist Aaron Beck suggested that fear and anxiety arise when the person 'senses' danger and they anticipate that they or a loved one could come to harm. Depression arises from a feeling that you have lost something important forever. You feel happy, in contrast, when you experience pleasure or expect a positive event.[6]

In other words, Beck believed, events do not *directly* cause anxiety, depression and other emotional problems. Rather, our interpretation of an event determines whether we develop anxiety, depression or another psychiatric problem. You view the same event in different ways depending on whether you are happy and relaxed or depressed and anxious. For instance, when you're depressed or anxious, you may interpret a minor difficulty, as 'proof' things are getting worse. Negative emotions and expectations feed off each other, exacerbating the depression or anxiety.[6]

Beck's theory forms the foundation of cognitive behavioural therapy (CBT), a widely used psychotherapy for anxiety and depression.[6] As Butler and McManus comment, CBT is 'based on the idea that thoughts, feelings and behaviour are so intimately related that changing one will change the others'. While your emotions, thoughts and behaviours are learned rather than innate, changing them directly is difficult. So CBT changes the way you think, helps you to find 'new ways of seeing things or developing new perspectives and testing these out'.[184]

Butler and McManus offer the example of a relationship ending. The person may, understandably, interpret the breakdown as meaning that he or she will not find another partner. The resulting depression and anxiety can make it difficult to get out and meet new people. CBT can help the person focus on the characteristics the last partner found attractive and that means he or she can still make friends.[184]

CBT in practice

CBT identifies feelings, thoughts and behaviours associated with your anxiety or depression. Some of these are appropriate and helpful. While CBT replaces counterproductive feelings, thoughts, behaviours and beliefs, it isn't the same as positive thinking. As Tallis notes in *How To Stop Worrying* (see Futher reading), unjustified positive thinking replaces 'one unrealistic thought with a different kind of unrealistic thought'. Similarly, taking responsibility is not the same as blaming yourself.

Your therapist may ask you to record negative thoughts and behaviours in a diary. You then work together to understand how these thoughts and behaviours trigger stress, anxiety, depression and so on. You can then look at the evidence for and against each thought and behaviour. Finally, you can replace counterproductive ideas with more objective and rational approaches, which helps you cope more effectively and efficiently. For instance, people with GAD (page 26) tend to regard ambiguous or neutral stimuli as potentially threatening. CBT helps people regard such stimuli more objectively.[89] CBT usually uses explicit objectives, broken into manageable, short-term goals and supported by regular 'homework'.

Often, you will find it hard to shift an idea even if you know that it provokes depression and anxiety. For instance, knowing that feeling terrified of a money spider, or of going to the supermarket, is absurd does not stop the panic attack. So, the therapist may suggest gradual desensitization. A person with agoraphobia may walk to the corner, then to the local shops, and then take a bus and so on. At first, they may venture out accompanied by someone. Once they gain confidence, they can go out on their own. A person with a phobia of spiders may be shown pictures, then one in a tank, then allow one to crawl over their hand.

Therapists may add other elements, such as mindfulness (page 63) and applied relaxation (page 113), which allows you to cope better when faced with a situation that provokes anxiety or when treatment makes you feel uncomfortable. Contact the British Association for Behavioural and Cognitive Psychotherapies.

How effective are the talking therapies?

Scientists have studied only a few of the 500 different psychotherapies and behavioural therapies. Furthermore, therapists often draw on several approaches to develop personalized programmes, which makes identifying effectiveness difficult. However, broadly, the 'conventional' approaches – such as CBT and psychoanalysis – seem to be equally effective. Anxiety and mood disorders may respond, some researchers believe, better to CBT than to psychodynamic treatments, such as Freudian and analytical psychoanalysis.[93] But the strength of the bond between therapist and client – the so-called therapeutic alliance – and their personalities seem to be more important than the type of therapy.[93] As you might expect, more experienced therapists tend to have the best results.

Effective therapists make you feel understood and engender trust. You and your therapist should clearly agree on the goals of therapy and identity a 'therapeutic pathway' outlining how you can overcome your difficulties. As mentioned above, you need to remain committed, even if you experience emotional and mental discomfort. So, the therapist should communicate hope and optimism, while acknowledging the severity and persistence of your difficulties.

You shouldn't feel the therapist is judging you, talking down to you or seems bored and disinterested. However, many people with depression and anxiety have been overlooked, rejected and victimized, so they may be 'hypersensitive' to actual or perceived criticism and disinterest. You need to be honest with yourself and work out if you are expecting this reaction even when it's not there. Try raising your concerns with the therapist before you switch.[15] If you find the right therapist, psychotherapy is highly effective, for instance:

- approximately 46 per cent of people with GAD show a clinically significant response to psychological therapies;[95]
- about 60 per cent of people with OCD (page 29) significantly improved after CBT;[4]
- approximately 75 per cent of those with PTSD (page 31) benefit from CBT;[4]
- CBT can be as effective as antidepressants for moderate to severe depression – in one study, after 8 weeks, depression improved in 50 per cent of those taking medications and 43 per cent of those receiving CBT, but just 25 per cent of those taking a placebo;[5]
- 46 per cent of adults in the UK who did not respond to antidepressants reported at least a 50 per cent reduction in depression six months after they also received CBT compared to 22 per cent of those managed with 'usual care', such as changing drugs or referral to psychiatric services.[96]

In other words, CBT improves outcomes even for people taking antidepressants. The treatments are complementary rather than alternatives.

Interpersonal therapy and family therapy

Many psychotherapies focus on the individual's capacity to change their thoughts, feelings and behaviours. They do not directly address wider problems that contribute to anxiety and depression, such as issues between people. In contrast, as its name suggests, interpersonal therapy focuses on the struggles, misunderstandings and other issues that develop between people. For example, some people with depression or anxiety are unable to develop or sustain meaningful relationships with family, friends and colleagues. This can undermine their defences against stress as well as leading to conflict. Interpersonal therapy can help bridge the gap that occurs between them and other people.

Family therapy can help resolve conflict and misunderstandings that can arise inside a family, which may contribute to anxiety and depression. Family therapy can help you deal with issues such as guilt, anger and embarrassment that arise *from* anxiety and depression. This reduces misunderstandings and fosters a family environment that aids recovery.[15]

Social skills and assertiveness training

Social skills training can help, for example, people start, maintain and end conversations. Social skills training also explores emotions, body language and tone of voice, which make important contributions to communication and social interactions. As such, social skills training can help people with social phobia (page 28), those who are withdrawn and those who didn't develop effective social skills when they were growing up.

Assertiveness training can help you stand up for your rights without causing undue anxiety. Not being able to say 'no' to unrealistic demands – such as those made at work or in a family – can cause stress or anxiety. Often unassertive people will ruminate thinking, 'Why didn't I say that?' or 'If only I'd done this', which can contribute to or arise from depression. You could start by making a list of situations where you would like to be more assertive. Think about what you fear might happen if you were assertive and consider how realistic the adverse outcomes might be. Many adult education centres run assertiveness training courses.

Mindfulness

Recently, mindfulness attracted considerable interest among doctors and therapists as a treatment for anxiety, depression and stress in its own right and combined with CBT. Some adult education centres now offer mindfulness courses. Definitions vary. Essentially, however, mindfulness training encourages you to concentrate, non-judgementally and openly, on the present rather than worry about what might happen or ruminate on the past. As we have seen, catastrophization and rumination are important and often difficult to resolve aspects of anxiety and depression. People with depression and anxiety tend to ruminate and catastrophize 'automatically'. Some therapists compare mindfulness to waking up from life on automatic pilot.

Against this background, mindfulness training allows you a step back from your anxiety, low mood, frustrations and other emotions. As such, mindfulness seems to increase your ability to regulate your behaviour, thoughts and emotions, as well as improving the flexibility of your thinking and enhancing attention. This helps you adapt more effectively to existing and future problems, clarify your issues, and identify and implement solutions.[97] For example, a stress-reduction programme that encompasses mindfulness typically lasts between eight and ten weeks and may use meditation to help you recognize and escape from habitual, counterproductive thoughts and behaviours.[98, 99]

You can try mindfulness for yourself. Focus on a single object, idea, subject or sensation. If your mind wanders off, bring it back to your focus.[97] Try not to get annoyed if you fail. This is often much more difficult than it sounds. Mindfulness also encourages you to become more aware of your body and its response to internal and external stimuli.[97] However, anxious people already tend to be sensitive to mental and physical changes. So, try not to become too obsessed with how you feel.

Clinical studies suggest that mindfulness-based interventions alleviate, among other ailments, chronic pain, anxiety, depression, eating disorders, and drug and alcohol abuse (page 89), and help people quit smoking (page 85). Indeed, mindfulness-based CBT may reduce the risk that depression will relapse as effectively as antidepressants, in some people at least. When researchers looked at 18 studies, they found that mindfulness seemed to produce a 'small to medium' reduction in the symptoms of anxiety and depression.[185] Furthermore, used alongside CBT, mindfulness helps people accept and tolerate the unpleasant emotions that the therapy or changing habitual behaviours may evoke.[98, 99]

Meditation and mindfulness

In many ways, mindfulness is similar to the meditation taught by Buddhism and some other Eastern religions – at least in the early stages of the training – and certain types of prayer, but stripped of religious connotations. Essentially, these differing techniques aim to calm the mind. Meditation is not confined to sitting in the lotus position for hours chanting 'om' or another mantra. Indeed, most people find it easier to be more intensely aware of their bodies while walking or moving. T'ai chi, qi gong, yoga and rosary prayer are also forms of meditation. Sahaja yoga, for example, emphasizes meditation that aims to create 'mental silence' or 'thoughtless awareness' rather than the physical postures and breathing exercises better known in the West. A review of 11 studies showed reductions in anxiety, depression and stress, as well as improvements in subjective and psychological well-being. Further studies are needed to determine the extent of the improvement, particularly in people with mental health disorders.[203] Learning classical meditation can be difficult without guidance; you could see if your local adult education centres hold courses. Your vicar or spiritual adviser will help you pray effectively.

Overcoming grief

Sometimes, we label emotions, events and mental states that are part of being human as like a disease. Grief, for example, following the death of a friend or relative, the end of a relationship or the loss of a job is almost inevitable. Indeed, some people recover from a relative's death more rapidly and fully than after being fired, possibly because there is less loss of self-esteem when someone dies.[15] Death comes to us all. But people who have lost their job often pick over their behaviour to see if they could have avoided being fired. They may also feel intensely guilty, especially if their families face financial hardship.

In such cases, some people feel tempted to resort to drugs – legal, illegal and prescription – to blunt grief's edge. But taking antidepressants could be counterproductive. For example, almost half of people who responded to antidepressants would not take them again because of the psychological side effects (page 43), such as narrowing of their emotional range, not feeling like themselves and an inability to cry.[44]

Yet a low mood, not feeling yourself and crying are all part of normal grieving. According to one estimate, 'resolving' the loss of a loved pet means crying for at least 20 hours. 'Resolving' (you may never overcome) the loss of a spouse, parent, child or close friend requires 200–300 hours of crying.[92] Even extreme reactions are normal: about half of widows and widowers interviewed in mid Wales reported hallucinations or illusions of their spouse.[100]

Most people begin to recover a few weeks or months after bereavement. However, bereavement is severely stressful and triggers major depression in about one in ten people.[101,102] Others develop debilitating 'complicated grief'. So, how can you tell the difference? Typically, grief comes in waves and you maintain self-esteem.[15] Depression produces persistent distress and undermines self-esteem.[103] Bereaved people are less likely to think about suicide than those with depression.[15] Bereaved people are also less likely to show slowed thinking and movements, or worry excessively about past actions.[15] Nevertheless, regrets are common.

People with complicated grief, in contrast, typically endure prolonged, intense sorrow. They yearn for the deceased. They may report frequent, intrusive thoughts and memories of the deceased.[102] People with complicated grief may experience intrusive thoughts or exhibit inappropriate behaviours and emotions. They can have difficulty comprehending the reality of the person's death or imagining a future with 'purpose and meaning'.[102] So, speak to your GP or a counsellor if several weeks after the death you:

- feel you have depression, PTSD (page 31) or complicated grief;
- start abusing drugs or alcohol;
- feel 'dead' or 'unreal';
- find you cannot work or take part in your normal activities.

Medicines, psychological interventions, such as guided mourning and practical support (e.g. for dealing with wills, money and benefits) can help. Cruse, the Child Bereavement Trust, and your church or spiritual adviser can also offer advice and support.

Solving the problem of problem solving

Unresolved personal problems can cause, exacerbate and perpetuate depression and anxiety. Indeed, Tallis remarks that worriers 'appear to be very good at defining problems, but extremely bad at solving them'. Worriers and people with anxiety tend to be slower at making decisions, possibly because they want to be absolutely sure that the decision is right. They're haunted by doubt. In particular, Tallis notes, worriers 'have unrealistically high evidence expectations'. In other words, 'they want to know exactly what is going to happen' if they take a course of action. However, we can make few – if any – decisions without an element of risk. If this sounds like you, a more active, planned approach to problem solving may help. First, you define your problems. Then you figure out a plan to tackle them. Finally, you break the plan into realistic short-term goals.

A form of psychotherapy called 'problem-solving therapy' takes this approach, using principles of CBT (page 60) either individually or in small groups over 7 to 14 sessions. The person and the therapist work together to, step-by-step, constructively identify, understand and prioritize the person's difficulties. Sessions focus on developing the problem-solving skills needed to reach a solution. As is typical with CBT, problem-solving therapy focuses on immediate and pressing difficulties and the approach seems to work. Researchers considered 11 studies, involving 2,072 people, with anxiety, depression or both. Overall, problem-solving therapy improved symptoms of anxiety and depression. Indeed, some people find that problem-solving therapy markedly improves their symptoms.[186]

Identifying your problems

Sometimes identifying your problem can pose a challenge, especially if you are in denial or repression. So, on a blank piece of paper, try to answer the following questions.

- What is the problem? Try to state the problem as a clear, simple sentence: 'The pressure at work is more than I can cope with'; 'I cannot control my drinking and the hangovers and guilt leaves me depressed and anxious'; 'I am anxious about my finances'. You can also home in on the fundamentals by considering what the problem is not, or when the problem arises: 'I do not drink unless I have to meet people'.
- Do you face more than one issue? If you cannot state the problem in a single sentence, you may have more than one issue. Try breaking the issue down or make a list of everything that bothers you. Then rewrite these as problems – in other words, phrased in a way that could be solved. So, 'I am always broke' and 'I am bored stiff at work' are issues. 'I haven't had a decent pay rise in two years' and 'I have been passed over for promotion and the work is now routine' are problems.

- Who contributes to the problem? List everyone who influences the problem or your ability to tackle the issue. Then consider who makes matters worse, who helps and whom you need to consider. You may want to move and make a 'fresh start' elsewhere. However, your children's school, your partner's job and your commitments to, for example, elderly parents may restrict your room for manoeuvre. Now ask yourself: 'What have I contributed?' Be honest. Most of us lay at least some of the blame at someone else's feet – a coping strategy called transference. On the other hand, try not to blame yourself for events outside your control or for the actions of others.
- Where and when does the problem occur? Understanding where and when a problem occurs can help uncover why it arises. Keeping a diary can reveal patterns, triggers and possible solutions. For example, assertiveness training may help if you drink to bolster your self-confidence or deal with social phobia. Relaxation therapy may help if you smoke because you are stressed. Adding exercise to your everyday activities (page 99) may help if you cannot find the time otherwise.

Some therapists suggest blocking an hour a week or so for 'problem solving'. It's worth doing if you can, at least for a few weeks. You could get out of the house: go to a café or library, for example. The change in environment and fewer distractions can help you focus. You could keep a 'worry journal' and jot down your concerns, problems and issues. You could also look back on – but try not to ruminate on – an event that upset you. Try to identify specifically what upset you.[21] Again, turn these thoughts, impressions and memories into problems, which helps identify solutions.

Finding solutions

Once you have identified a problem, ask yourself what about it bothers you the most.[21] If you have more than one issue, rank these in the terms of the most pressing, the most easily solved, or the most important. The most pressing might be your inability to perform well when you have to give a presentation. The most easily solved might be to go down the gym more often. The most important might be to follow your true vocation. Successfully tackling simple problems, even if relatively trivial, gives you the confidence to deal with more difficult, more important issues.

Now write down as many solutions as possible: no matter how absurd, no matter how impractical, no matter how bizarre. Robbing a bank would solve your financial problems. However, it's hardly realistic. Yet 'thinking the unthinkable' sets a boundary that allows you to find as many options as possible. You can get rid of the impractical, unrealistic and illegal ones later. Management consultants who advise companies about creativity like to point out that during this process 'There is no such thing as a bad idea': problem solving should be an intellectual and emotional free for all. Write the ideas down, which can help you translate a vague idea into a more concrete proposal. I would suggest that you keep the diary to yourself or password protect the file if you are making notes on your computer or smartphone.

You could rank the pros and cons of each solution on a scale – many people use 1 to 10. As Tallis comments in *How To Stop Worrying* (see Futher reading), assigning values helps you consider the consequences thoroughly. But even if the evidence seems overwhelming, do not ignore your gut instinct. If something still feels wrong, it probably is. So, if you feel able to, talk it over. At least think about it again. Your gut feeling might be telling you that you haven't considered all the options.

Once you're happy with your solution, develop a plan to move from theory to practice. Ideally, break this down into short-term (with deadlines), manageable goals. Then track your progress against these deadlines.

Distinguish between wants and needs

You may need to differentiate between what you *think* you want or need and what you *really* want and need. Tallis remarks that this is the difference between self and self-concept. The self is the real you. The self-concept is the impression of 'you' that you derive from other people's expectations and values. You may need to ask yourself who you are taking the decision for – yourself or someone else. Of course, there are many times in life when you take decisions for other people. However, your true self can become submerged in expectations and values derived from other people. This can cause considerable stress and, in turn, anxiety and depression.

Bibliotherapy

Bibliotherapy uses books to help you solve or better understand your issues. You may find that reading biographies, such as those by William Styron and Richard Mabey (see Further reading), describing how other people survived their crises, helps. Reading literary fiction helps you explore and understand your problems. You could also jot down inspiring passages. Of course, reading light fiction can help you focus on something other than your problems. Ask your local library if there is a 'bibliotherapy' group near you.

Several studies suggest that self-help guides can alleviate depression as effectively as CBT. The person reads the book or uses a computer-based CBT programme (see below). In some studies, a CBT therapist offers advice over the phone, such as a call once a week lasting between 5 and 15 minutes.[1] In a study from Glasgow, depression severity halved in 43 per cent of patients after four months of treatment with a self-help book and, on average, two face-to-face sessions each lasting about 40 minutes. Only 26 per cent of those receiving usual care reported a halving in symptom severity. Overall, following the advice in the self-help book approximately doubled the chances of recovery from depression after four months and the benefits seemed to persist for at least a year.[104]

However, there is a risk that a person will embark on bibliotherapy without a proper diagnosis.[1] Do not rely on bibliotherapy alone if you are having a bad time or nervous breakdown, you are thinking about suicide or self-harm, or are heavily abusing drugs or alcohol.

Whether you read a book or see a therapist you need to stick with the programme and implement the suggestions. Only half of a group of people who started a bibliotherapy programme for phobia finished, for example. However, when researchers looked at six studies they found that, on average, 7 per cent of people with depression stopped bibliotherapy, compared to 3 per cent of those undergoing conventional therapy.[1] So, bibliotherapy might be better for certain conditions than others.

Online CBT

Some people find that internet-based CBT helps. Indeed, NICE now recommends computerized CBT for some people, such as those with persistent subthreshold or mild to moderate depression. The choice of approach – face to face with telephone support or using a computer – depends largely on your preference. One study assessed an online course that included elements of mindfulness-based stress reduction and cognitive therapy for stress, anxiety and depression. The programme consisted of ten sessions, guided meditation videos and automated emails. Users completed the course, at a pace they set themselves, over at least four weeks. Perceived stress, depression and GAD significantly decreased at the end of the course and decreased further a month later. The benefit was similar to other face-to-face and online interventions.[105]

Another study combined results from 14 studies looking at web- or computer-based treatments for psychological problems among students. Computer-delivered interventions improved depression by 57 per cent, anxiety by 44 per cent and stress by 27 per cent compared to no treatment.[106] However, check who funded the site and make sure that it comes from a reputable source. There is no universal quality control on the web.

5

Eat to beat depression and anxiety

It's hard, but many people with anxiety and depression benefit from sticking to a routine, such as having a regular sleep pattern (page 120), not drinking too much caffeine (page 94) or alcohol (page 89), taking exercise (page 99)[15] and eating a healthy diet. Indeed, a diet high in vegetables, fruit, meat, fish and whole grains seems to protect against depression and anxiety compared to filling up on processed and fried food, refined grains and sugar-laden snacks.

Unfortunately, many people with depression and anxiety lack the motivation to eat healthily. They may grab fat- or sugar-laden snacks – such as chocolate, biscuits and cakes – to try to make them feel better. They might not be able to motivate themselves to eat well. Poor diet and a generally unhealthy lifestyle seem to explain to an extent why the risk of premature death is higher in people with depression than the general population.[187] Many people with depression seek temporary solace in alcohol, nicotine or street drugs. They may neglect their basic needs, such as a healthy diet, and are vulnerable to accidental injuries.

A Canadian study followed 3,410 adults for mostly 19 years. On average, people with depression had shorter life expectancies. For example, among adults who doctors started following in 1992, average life expectancy at 25 years of age was 18.6 years shorter in depressed women and 7.6 years shorter in depressed men than in people without depression. 'The association between depression and mortality persists over long periods of time and has emerged among women in recent decades, despite contemporaneous improvements in the treatment of depression and reduction of stigma associated with depression', the authors comment.[187]

The increased risk of death associated with depression may reflect the 'cumulative impact' of risky behaviours, such as poor-quality diet, smoking, alcohol abuse and lack of exercise. The association between depression and mortality tended to weaken over time – unless the person endured a relapse. The researchers comment that 'remission from depression (either spontaneously or due to treatment) can reverse the elevated risk of mortality otherwise associated with depression'.[187]

Diet may also directly influence the risk of depression and anxiety: low levels of nutrients can affect how well our brains work. In other words, it is easy to become trapped in a spiral where depression and anxiety lead to poor food choices, which can leave you even more low and wound up, and so on.[21]

This chapter looks at some elements of a healthy diet that can help anxiety and depression. Apart from bolstering your defences, the dietary changes could enhance the effectiveness of psychotherapy and improve your responses to antidepressants or anxiolytics, and may even allow a reduction in dose. However, as we have mentioned several times, never stop or reduce the dose of your drug without speaking to your doctor first, even if you feel better. If you take a MAOI always check before changing your diet.

Some people find certain supplements help their anxiety and depression. If you suffer from a serious disease, or are taking one or more medicines, check with a pharmacist or a doctor that the supplement is safe. The government regularly reviews the safe doses and the recommended daily intake, so always check NHS Choices before taking supplements.

A reputable multi-vitamin is likely to follow the government's and other official recommendations. However, there are also numerous herbal (page 115) and other supplements available in shops and on the net. So, always check with your doctor or a dietician that these are safe and read as much as you can about the supplement. Some can have side effects, especially if you are taking other medicines or use a high dose. Stop taking the supplement if you feel unwell.

Minerals and trace elements

A vitamin is made by the living world – a plant, animal or your skin, which makes vitamin D, for example. Minerals are not. Your body needs tiny amounts of iron, zinc, magnesium and other trace elements (minerals) for health and well-being. For instance, many trace elements influence transmission between nerves that are involved in emotions, and modulate levels of neurotransmitters including serotonin and noradrenaline.[107] We need trace elements in our diets in tiny amounts. You should get all you need from a healthy, balanced diet. Yet many people don't get enough, which might contribute to anxiety and depression. You also need vitamins and minerals for optimal health and well-being. So, while I try to eat a healthy diet, I also take a supplement of vitamins and minerals as an 'insurance' policy.

Magnesium

Magnesium is involved in about 300 chemical reactions that keep us alive, including ensuring that:

- our muscles and nerves work properly;
- our blood pressure remains within safe limits;
- our hearts beat normally;
- we have sufficient energy;
- our bones stay healthy (bones contain about 50 to 60 per cent of the 25 grams of magnesium in an adult's body).

According to the NHS, men need 300 milligrams magnesium a day, while women need 270 milligrams. So, try eating magnesium-rich foods, such as spinach, legumes, nuts, seeds and whole grains. As a rule, high-fibre foods are rich in magnesium. Food processing – such as stripping away the germ and bran – cuts magnesium levels by up to 90 per cent.[108] So, look for whole grains (page 80). Some breakfast cereals, and mineral and bottled waters contain magnesium – so read the label (Table 5.1).

Patients deficient in magnesium are susceptible to anxiety, depression and suicide.[107] Some people find magnesium supplements alleviate their depression and anxiety. In experimental animals, magnesium

Table 5.1 Magnesium-rich foods

Food	Serving size	Amount of magnesium in a serving (milligrams)
Almonds, dry roasted	1 ounce (28 grams)	80
Spinach, boiled	1 ounce (28 grams)	78
Cashews, dry-roasted	1 ounce (28 grams)	74
Peanuts, oil-roasted	¼ cup (38 grams)	63
Soy milk	1 cup (half a pint)	61
Black beans, cooked	½ cup (31 grams)	60
Peanut butter, smooth	2 tablespoons	49
Bread, whole wheat	2 slices	46
Avocado, cubed	1 cup (225 grams)	44
Potato, baked with skin	3.5 ounces (99 grams)	43
Rice, brown, cooked	½ cup (95 grams)	42
Yogurt, low-fat, plain	8 ounces (227 grams)	42

Source Adapted from <http//ods.od.nih.gov/factsheets/Magnesium-HealthProfessional> and converted from US measures supplements alleviate depressive- and anxiety-like symptoms, improve mental deficits, and augment the effectiveness of some antidepressants.[107] So, some people try magnesium supplements. The NHS warns that taking more than 400 milligrams a day of magnesium can cause diarrhoea and the long-term effects of taking high doses – if any – aren't known.

Zinc

Zinc, among other essential actions, helps the body make proteins and allows cells to divide normally. In addition, depressed and anxious people seem to have lower zinc levels in their blood than healthy people. Zinc deficiency also seems to impair antidepressants' efficacy. On the other hand, animal studies suggest that zinc supplements improve depression, augment antidepressants' effectiveness and shorten the time before symptoms improve. In one study, 60 patients with difficult-to-treat major depression received imipramine once daily and either placebo or zinc supplements (25 milligrams a day) for 12 weeks. Zinc supplements reduced the severity of the depression.[107]

According to the NHS, men (aged 19–64 years) need about 9.5 milligrams of zinc a day and women (aged 19–64 years) about 7 milligrams daily. Good sources of zinc include red meat, seafood, nuts, beans, and whole grains.[107] However, large amounts of zinc reduce the amount of copper we absorb, which can lead to anaemia and weaken bones. So, the NHS suggests not taking more than 25 milligrams of zinc supplements a day, unless advised by a doctor.

Iron

Low levels of iron means that the blood carries less oxygen. This can leave you feeling weak, tired and lethargic. Healthy cells need iron to function normally and to produce DNA and neurotransmitters. Low iron levels can alter mood and behaviour, and trigger depression.[107] The NHS suggests that men older than 18 years and women older than 50 years need 8.7 milligrams of iron a day. Women aged between 19 and 50 years need 14.8 milligrams a day. Women who lose a lot of blood during their periods may need to take supplements. So, try to eat enough iron, particularly from red meat, poultry and fish. Do not drink tea, which binds iron, with meals. Taking a supplement containing 17 milligrams or less iron a day is, the NHS says, unlikely to cause harm. Higher levels can cause constipation, nausea, vomiting and stomach pain. Very high levels of iron can prove harmful, and even fatal, for young children. So, always keep iron supplements out of their reach.

Selenium

Low levels of selenium are linked with depression and 'other negative mood states', the British Dietetic Association remarks. You need, according to the NHS, about 0.075 milligrams of selenium a day for men (aged 19–64 years) and 0.06 milligrams for women (aged 19–64 years). You should get this from a healthy diet that includes nuts, meat, fish, seeds and wholemeal bread.

The NHS says that a supplement containing up to 0.35 milligrams of selenium a day is unlikely to cause harm. However, higher doses can cause 'selenosis', which even when mild can lead to loss of hair, skin and nails.

Chromium

Animal studies suggest that several chromium salts – including chromium picolinate and chromium chloride – may counter depression. In humans, studies suggest, chromium picolinate alleviated major and atypical depression, and premenstrual dysphoric disorder.[107]

Adults need approximately 0.025 milligrams of chromium a day. Good sources include broccoli, brewer's yeast, beef, eggs, liver, oysters and chicken.

The NHS comments that the effects of regularly taking high doses are not known. However, up to 10 milligrams a day from food and supplements is, the NHS says, unlikely to cause harm.

The B vitamins

To stay healthy, we need adequate levels of 13 essential vitamins including at least 8 members of the 'B' group. Again, you need tiny amounts: you need about 25 grams of thiamin (vitamin B_1) during your life.[108] But you can't live without them. For instance, low levels of vitamin B_1, niacin (B_3) or cobalamin (B_{12}) seem to contribute to tiredness and feeling depressed or irritable, the British Dietetic Association warns. Boost your intake by eating more fortified foods, wholegrain cereals, meat, fish, eggs and dairy. Low amounts of folate (vitamin B_9) may increase the chance of feeling depressed. In one investigation of 2,313 men aged between 42 and 60 years, low levels of folate trebled the risk of developing depression over, on average, the next 13 years.[109]

In addition, people with depression and anxiety often eat a poor diet, take drugs or drink excessive amounts of alcohol, all of which can lower folate.[47] So, it's especially important for people with depression and anxiety to get enough folate from sources such as liver, green vegetables, oranges and other citrus fruits, beans, and fortified foods – such as yeast extract (Marmite) and some breakfast cereals (read the labels).

People with depression who tire rapidly may be especially likely to benefit from eating more folate-rich foods or taking a supplement.[47]

Fish

Vitamin D

Generations of children dreaded the daily spoonful of cod liver oil, which is a great source of vitamins A and D. Their parents forced it down to prevent rickets. We know that low levels of vitamin D also increase the risk of experiencing depression.[110] In the winter, we make less vitamin D from sunlight, which might contribute to seasonal affective disorder (page 10).

According to NICE, about a fifth of adults and 8 to 24 per cent of children in the UK have levels of vitamin D below those that support bone health. Vitamin D deficiency is particularly common in certain groups. For example, from 82 to 94 per cent of people of south Asian origin living in the UK may be vitamin D deficient in the summer and winter respectively. Several factors contribute, including darker skin that limits synthesis, attire that covers the body and traditional diets low in vitamin D.[188]

Oily fish is the only significant dietary source of vitamin D in the UK. Egg yolk, red meat and fortified foods provide small amounts. Sunlight that reaches the UK from October to the beginning of April does not contain the UV wavelength that synthesizes vitamin D. During these months, we depend on reserves of vitamin D accumulated during the summer, which clearly is often insufficient. So, the NHS suggests that everyone (including pregnant and breastfeeding women) should take a supplement containing 10 micrograms of vitamin D daily during the autumn and winter. Vulnerable people are advised to take vitamin D supplements year-round.[189] Vulnerable groups are:

- children less than 4 years of age
- pregnant and breastfeeding women, particularly teenagers and young women
- people more than 65 years of age
- people who have low or no sun exposure, including those who cover their skin, are housebound or confined indoors for long periods
- people with darker skin (such as those of African, African-Caribbean or south Asian origin)
- some people eating particular diets, such as those who avoid nuts or follow vegan, halal or kosher diets.

Omega-3 fatty acids

Fish oil contains about 50 different fats. The omega-3 fatty acids are among the most important of these, contributing to memory, intellectual performance, healthy vision, healthy joints and various other health benefits. Omega-3 fatty acids are, for instance, the main reason why eating fish once or twice a week protects against heart disease.

EPA (eicosapentaenoic acid) and DHA (docosahexaenoic acid), the two main omega-3 fatty acids, also seem to counter depression. Patients taking a drug called interferon-alpha to treat persistent infection with hepatitis C virus, which attacks the liver, can develop depression as a side effect. So, researchers treated people with purified EPA and DHA or a placebo for two weeks before starting interferon-alpha. Over the next six months, 30 per cent of those taking a placebo developed depression, which emerged after, on average, about 5 weeks. People taking DHA showed a similar risk of depression (28 per cent). However, symptoms took longer to emerge (about 12 weeks) compared to those given a placebo. EPA reduced the number of people with depression (10 per cent) and delayed onset (12 weeks).[111]

In 2014, delegates to the European College of Neuropsychopharmacology congress in Berlin heard that eating fatty fish appears to enhance responses to antidepressants. People with depression received an SSRI for 6 weeks and, if they did not respond, the authors gradually increased the dose. People with depression who ate fatty fish at least once a week had a 75 per cent chance of responding to antidepressants. Those who never ate fatty fish had only a 23 per cent chance of responding to antidepressants.

We can make omega-3 fatty acids from another fat (alpha-linolenic acid) in green leafy vegetables, nuts, seeds and their oils. But, it is a slow process. So, eating fish and seafood high in omega-3 fatty acids boosts levels of this essential nutrient (Table 5.2). The British Dietetic Association advises that adults, and children over 12 years of age, should eat two portions of fish per week (a portion is about 140 grams once cooked). One of these meals should be an oily fish. Omega-3 fatty acid levels are highest in fresh fish. Check the label of canned fish to make sure processing has not depleted the omega-3 oils. You can also check that the fish comes from sustainable stocks (<www.mcsuk.org>).

If you do not like the taste of oily fish, do not give up without trying some different fish and a few recipes. There are plenty of suggestions in cookbooks and on the internet (see, for example, <www.thefish society.co.uk>). For an island nation, our tastes in fish are remarkably conservative. If you really cannot stomach oily fish, you could try a

Table 5.2 Fish and seafood high in omega-3 fatty acids

Anchovy
Black cod (sablefish)
Crab
Dogfish (rock salmon)
Halibut
Herring
Mackerel
Mussels
Oysters
Pilchards
Rainbow trout
Sardines
Salmon
Tuna (especially bluefin)

Source Adapted from the University of Michigan and the British Dietetic Association

supplement. Speak to your doctor first if you are taking other medicines or have a chronic disease. If you have diabetes, for instance, omega-3 supplements may increase blood sugar levels.

Vegetables, fruit and fibre

Our ancestors fished, hunted and ate vegetables, legumes, fruits and whole grains, usually fresh and often raw. This traditional diet is high in fibre and rich in vitamins, minerals and other nutrients. The typical hunter-gatherers ate around five times more vitamin C than the average modern person, for instance.[108] As with magnesium, levels of vitamins and minerals are much lower in processed foods. This lack of essential nutrients might help explain why eating processed foods makes anxiety and depression more likely compared to eating a diet high in fruit, vegetables and wholegrain foods.[107]

Five portions of fruit and vegetables

Most nutritionists say we should eat at least five portions of fruits and vegetables a day – but some believe we should eat more. One portion weighs about 80 grams (Table 5.3). Certainly, fruits and vegetables are excellent sources of the nutrients that seem to tackle depression and anxiety. Cooking can leach nutrients. So, either eat fruit raw or cook vegetables using a small amount of unsalted water for as short a time as possible, lightly steam or stir-fry. Scrub rather than peel potatoes, carrots and so on: the skin often contains valuable nutrients.

Table 5.3 One portion of fruit or vegetables

One medium-sized fruit (banana, apple, pear, orange)
One slice of a large fruit (melon, pineapple, mango)
Two smaller fruits (plums, satsumas, apricots, peaches)
A dessert bowl full of salad
Three heaped tablespoons of vegetables
Three heaped tablespoons of pulses (chickpeas, lentils, beans)
Two to three tablespoons ('a handful') of grapes or berries
One tablespoon of dried fruit
One glass (150 millilitres) of unsweetened fruit or vegetable juice or smoothie
(two or more glasses of juice a day still counts as one portion)

Whole grains

Whole grains are an especially rich source of nutrients, some of which seem to help tackle depression and anxiety. Grains – the seeds of cereals such as wheat, rye, barley, oats and rice – have three areas.

- Bran, the outer layer, is rich in fibre and packed with nutrients. Bran covers the 'germ' and endosperm.
- The germ develops into a new plant. Wheat germ, for example, contains high levels of vitamin E, folate, zinc and magnesium, some of which protect against depression.
- The central endosperm is high in starch and provides the energy the germ needs to develop into a new plant.

Food manufacturers often refine grains by stripping off the bran and germ, and keeping the white endosperm. However, whole grains contain up to 75 per cent more nutrients than refined cereals, the British Dietetic Association points out. You should eat two to three servings daily. Nevertheless, about 95 per cent of adults in the UK do not eat enough whole grains. Nearly a third do not eat any. Try eating more foods with 'whole' in front of the grain's name – such as wholewheat pasta and whole oats.

Seeds, nuts and legumes

Seeds, nuts and legumes are another excellent source of nutrients. Peas, lentils, chickpeas and string beans contain up to twice the levels of vitamins and minerals as cereals, for example, and are rich in iron, zinc, selenium, magnesium, manganese, copper and nickel. As we have seen, some of these vitamins and minerals protect against anxiety and depression. However, plants use energy stored in seeds to aid the plant's growth and development. So, seeds and nuts are relatively high in calories. Try some vegetarian cookbooks: the right recipes will appeal to the palate of the most ardent carnivore!

Pro- and prebiotics

Pro- and prebiotics are mainstays of many pharmacies' supplement shelves. Further along the high street, supermarkets sell numerous probiotic yogurts and shakes. (Probiotics contain live bacteria, whereas prebiotics include nutrients that stimulate the growth or activity of specific bacteria.)

We've known for a while that the bacteria (microbiota) in the gut, for instance, control levels of dangerous bacteria (which is why antibiotics can cause diarrhoea), break down plant fibre and produce nutrients including vitamin B_{12}, thiamine, biotin, riboflavin, vitamin K and amino acids.[190] Gut bacteria also metabolize (break down) at least 50 drugs and other foreign chemicals.[191]

Over recent years, researchers increasingly recognized that the bacteria in our gut and other parts of the body influences numerous aspects of human biology, including digestion, the immune system and responses to certain drugs. Now increasing evidence links the microbiome's composition with several psychiatric and neurological disorders and diseases including autism, schizophrenia, attention deficit hyperactivity disorder, Parkinson's disease, Alzheimer's disease and multiple sclerosis.[192, 193] The recognition of the microbiome's potential importance inspired a new therapeutic strategy that uses live microorganisms to improve mental health.[194] Indeed, a recent study offers 'the first evidence' that probiotics 'may help reduce negative thoughts associated with sad mood'.[195]

Essentially, the human microbiome occupies five niches: the lower gastrointestinal tract, skin, mouth, nose and vagina. The diverse population of gastrointestinal bacteria release numerous signalling molecules that may influence the brain and behaviour.[192] Indeed, depressed patients, for example, show marked changes in the composition of their gastrointestinal microbiome.[192, 193]

Transplanting this abnormal microbiome may even 'transplant' depression. For instance, researchers transplanted faecal microbiotas from 34 depressed patients and 33 healthy controls into rats that had their gastrointestinal bacteria depleted by using a cocktail of antibiotics. Rats that received a transplant from depressed patients showed a dysregulated microbiota and exhibited anhedonia and anxiety-related behaviours compared to those that received a transplant from controls.[193, 195]

More recently, evidence emerged that some probiotics induce beneficial changes in humans, although further studies are needed. For instance, one study enrolled 22 healthy volunteers, who received a placebo and then *Bifidobacterium longum* 1714 daily, both for four weeks. The volunteers underwent a test that combined psychological and physiological stress, at baseline and after treatment. *B. longum* 1714 seemed to attenuate the increases in cortisol (a stress hormone) and anxiety induced by the test compared to an inactive placebo. Consuming the psychobiotic also seemed to reduce daily stress reported by the volunteers.[194]

Another study assessed a probiotic containing eight strains of bacteria. The study enrolled 40 healthy people without mood disorders who took the probiotic or a placebo once daily for four weeks. Compared to those who received the placebo, those who received the probiotic showed significantly reduced overall reactivity to sad mood, a trait that indicates vulnerability to depression. Reductions in rumination and aggressive thoughts accounted for most of the probiotic's benefits. These were people with anxiety or depression. Nevertheless, the authors concluded that 'These results provide the first evidence that the intake of probiotics may help reduce negative thoughts associated with sad mood'.[195]

Another approach uses prebiotics – in other words, nutrients that stimulate the growth or activity of specific bacteria. For instance, in mice, a combination of improved depression-like and anxiety-related behaviours that were induced by chronic stress responded to prebiotics.[193]

Current studies of probiotics and prebiotics in the treatment of anxiety and depression are, however, relatively small, with a short follow-up and typically enrolled healthy volunteers or else are based on responses in animals. So, while the results are promising, whether or not probiotics and prebiotics could become a new treatment for anxiety or depression remains uncertain and further studies are needed. If, however, you want to try a probiotic, such as *B. longum* 1714, speak to staff at your local healthfood shop or a pharmacist and be sure to follow the instructions.

Dieting to lose weight

Excess weight causes or contributes to numerous serious ailments including heart disease, type 2 diabetes, some cancers and depression. When researchers combined the results from 15 studies, obese people were 55 per cent more likely to develop depression than those of a healthy weight. Being overweight increased the risk by 27 per cent. The relationship runs both ways. People who were depressed were 58 per cent more likely to become obese.[40]

Weight itself is not a very good guide to your risk of developing depression and other disorders. Weighing 14 stone is fine if you are 6 foot 5. However, if you weighed 14 stone and were 5 foot 6, you would be seriously obese. Body mass index (BMI) takes your height and weight into account and so offers a better indication of whether your health is at risk. (To calculate your BMI, see <www.nhs.uk/Tools/Pages/Healthyweightcalculator.aspx>).

Try to keep your BMI between 18.5 and 24.9 kg/m². Below this and you are dangerously underweight. A BMI between 25.0 and 29.9 kg/m² suggests that you are overweight. You are probably obese if your BMI exceeds 30.0 kg/m². However, BMI may overestimate body fat in athletes, bodybuilders, hod carriers and other muscular people. Equally, BMI may underestimate body fat in older people and those who have lost muscle.

Doctors and gyms use monitors to check your body fat. However, not all fat is equal. Abdominal obesity damages your health more than fat elsewhere in your body. So, waist size can indicate whether or not your health is at risk (Table 5.4, overleaf).

Tips to help you lose weight

Unfortunately, losing weight is not easy – whatever the latest fad diets would have you believe. After all, millions of years of evolution drive us to consume food in times of feast, to help us survive times of famine. And you cannot stop eating as you can quit smoking or drinking alcohol. However, the following tips may help.

- Record *everything* you eat and drink for a couple of weeks. It is often easy to see where you inadvertently pile on extra calories: the odd biscuit, the occasional snack on chocolate or chips, the extra glass of wine or full-fat latte. It soon adds up.
- Use the BMI calculator to set a realistic, specific target. Rather than saying that you want to lose weight, resolve to lose two stone.

Table 5.4 Waist sizes linked to health risk

	Health at risk	Health at high risk
Men	Over 94 cm (37 inches)	Over 102 cm (40 inches)
Women	Over 80 cm (32 inches)	Over 88 cm (35 inches)
South Asian men		Over 90 cm (36 inches)
South Asian women		Over 80 cm (32 inches)

Source Adapted from the British Heart Foundation

Cutting between 500 and 1,000 calories each day can reduce body-weight by between 0.5 and 1.0 kilograms each week.[112]

- Think about how you tried to lose weight in the past. What techniques and diets worked? Which failed or proved impossible to stick to? Did a support group help?
- Do not let a slip-up derail your diet. Try to identify why you indulged. What were the triggers? Did you comfort eat to alleviate anxiety, stress or depression? Once you know why you slipped you can take steps to stop the problem.
- Begin your diet when you are at home over a weekend, or a holiday at home, and you do not have a celebration (such as Christmas or a birthday) planned. It is tougher beginning a diet on a Monday morning or when you are away in a hotel faced with fat-laden food, caffeine-rich drinks and alcohol.

If this fails, talk to your GP or pharmacist. Several medicines may help kick-start your weight loss. You can also try CBT (page 60), which can reduce weight by around 6 lbs (2.75 kilograms). Adding hypnosis (page 110) to CBT can increase weight loss to almost 15 lbs (6.75 kilograms).[113] None of these approaches offers a magic cure and you will still need to change your lifestyle. However, they help put you on the right course to breaking the link between anxiety, depression and weight.

6

The helpers that don't

Over the years, our ancestors tried drugging anxiety, depression and stress into submission with, for example, alcohol, nicotine, cannabis and opium. Despite modern medicines and psychotherapy, many people with depression and anxiety still self-medicate using street drugs, alcohol or nicotine – sometimes all three. These may help for a while, but withdrawal can trigger anxiety, stress and depression, as well as many other health problems. They are also highly addictive, expensive and directly (street drugs) or indirectly (violence and driving after drinking) illegal. So, users can face financial hardship and legal problems, which exacerbate stress, anxiety and depression. The helpers soon become part of the problem.

Unless you have struggled with being hooked on a legal or illegal drug, it is easy to dismiss addiction, dependency and heavy use as lifestyle choices. However, addiction erodes the person's ability to say no. The compulsion to use the drug overwhelms their good intentions and breaks down every intellectual, rational and emotional defence that the user can muster.

Smoking

Nicotine, tobacco's addictive chemical, and the plant's scientific name (*Nicotiana tabacum*) 'honour' Jean Nicot de Villemain (1530–1600), a sixteenth-century French ambassador to Portugal. Villemain introduced tobacco to fashionable Parisian society when he returned from Lisbon in 1561. However, concerns that smoking harmed health soon emerged. In 1604, James I of England (James VI of Scotland) described smoking as 'loathsome to the eye, hateful to the nose, harmful to the brain, and dangerous to the lungs'.

According to Action on Smoking and Health (ASH), smoking in Great Britain peaked in 1948 when 82 per cent of men smoked. By 1974, 45 per cent of adults smoked. Recent figures suggest that smoking continues to decline in popularity. According to the Smoking Toolkit Study, 24 per cent of adults smoked during 2007, falling to about 17 per cent in 2018.

> ### Illegal drugs, anxiety and depression
>
> Depression and anxiety increase the likelihood of using illegal and legal mind-altering drugs. In one study, depressed people tended to use cocaine and alcohol rather than other drugs (such as cannabis, amphetamine and opiates) to self-medicate: cocaine dependence started almost 7 years after the first episode of depression. In drug users, alcohol dependence emerged about four-and-a-half years after the first bout of depression.[114] Another study found that 1 in every 33 people with specific phobias and panic disorder without agoraphobia self-medicate with illegal drugs combined with alcohol.[115]
>
> If you use illegal drugs to self-medicate, you need help. Apart from the harm you may do yourself, a run in with the legal system will make matters worse. If you abuse drugs, speak to your GP, contact your local drug treatment services (<www.talktofrank.com/need-support>) or call the FRANK helpline on 0300 123 6600.

Smokers gamble with their health

Smoking caused 86 per cent of lung cancers in the UK in 2010 as well as, among other malignancies: 65 per cent of cancers in the mouth, throat and oesophagus; 29 per cent of pancreatic cancers; and 22 per cent of stomach cancers.[116] Overall, smokers are roughly twice as likely to die from cancer as non-smokers. Smoking also makes heart disease and stroke more likely. When researchers combined results from 81 studies involving almost 4 million people, smoking increased the risk of ischaemic stroke (caused by a blocked blood vessel) by 54 and 53 per cent in women and men, respectively. Smoking also increased the risk of haemorrhagic stroke (bleeding into the brain) by 63 and 22 per cent, respectively.[117]

Quitting will reduce your likelihood of developing most of the smoking-related diseases. A person who stops smoking at 40 years of age will gain, on average, 9 years of life. Even a 60-year-old will gain 3 years.

Mood disturbances – such as depression, anxiety, stress and anger – commonly trigger smokers to light up.[118] An overview of 15 studies, for instance, concluded that anxiety disorders increased the risk of regular smoking by 41 per cent and nicotine dependence by 58 per cent.[119] Interestingly, quitting smoking reduces depression, anxiety and stress, and improves mood and quality of life. Indeed, quitting smoking can be as or more effective than antidepressants in people with depression, anxiety or both.[120]

The dangers to your family

If the physical and psychological benefits are not enough to make you quit, think about the harm smoking does to your loved ones. Second-hand smoke contains more than 4,000 chemicals, including about 50 carcinogens – cancer-causing agents. This chemical cocktail increases the risk that people who inhale second-hand smoke will develop serious diseases, including cancer, heart disease, asthma and sudden infant death syndrome. For example, a woman who lives with a smoker is 24 and 30 per cent more likely to develop lung cancer and heart disease respectively than lifelong non-smokers. Over a lifetime, passive smokers inhale a similar amount of fine particle 'pollution' as non-smokers living in heavily polluted cities.[121]

Making quitting easier

On some measures, nicotine is more addictive than heroin or cocaine. As a result, fewer than 1 in 30 smokers quit annually and more than half relapse within a year, partly because of the intense withdrawal symptoms, which include feeling irritable, restless and anxious, insomnia and intensely craving a cigarette. These symptoms generally abate over two weeks or so. If you cannot tough it out, nicotine replacement therapy (NRT) 'tops up' your nicotine levels, without exposing you to the other harmful chemicals, which reduces withdrawal symptoms. So, NRT alleviates the discomfort and increases your chance of quitting by between 50 and 100 per cent. You need to find the right combination of NRT for you.

- Patches reduce withdrawal symptoms for 16 to 24 hours. However, patches have a slow onset of action.
- Nicotine chewing gum, lozenges, inhalers and nasal spray act more quickly, but do not last as long.

Talk to your pharmacist or GP. Doctors can prescribe other treatments, such as bupropion and varenicline, that aid cessation.

E-cigarettes

Electronic cigarettes (also called vaping) also seem to help you quit. In part, ASH suggests, their success may reflect e-cigarettes' ability to replicate smoking's superficial aspects. Even placebo e-cigarettes reduce cravings, alleviate withdrawal and cut cigarette consumption. The wide range of e-cigarettes means that you should be able to find one that suits you.

E-cigarettes can cause mouth and throat irritation, however, and any long-term side effects are poorly characterized. So it is best to use e-cigarettes to stop, rather than replace, smoking. The risks from passive vaping are not fully understood and it might be prudent to also limit passive exposure as far as practical.

Tips to help you quit

NRT and e-cigarettes can help. But you need to be motivated and you may need to tackle your depression or anxiety before your nicotine addiction. Many smokers find that a low mood and a lack of confidence pose important barriers to quitting. On the other hand, a positive mood at the start of the quit attempt makes cessation more likely.[118] Indeed, doctors in some countries prescribe bupropion as an antidepressant and anxiolytic as well as a smoking cessation aid.

Some smokers recognize that lighting up is a 'learned reaction' to a mood disturbance even though they now gain 'little relief' from the tobacco. Smoking seems to offer smokers a 'sense of control' and a way to 'fill a void created by a lack of meaningful activities'.[118] So, find something that takes your mind off smoking. If you find yourself smoking when you get home in the evening, try a new hobby, exercise (page 99) or active relaxation (page 113). If you find car journeys boring without a cigarette, try an audio book. Most ex-smokers find that the craving for a cigarette usually only lasts a couple of minutes.

Keeping a diary of problems and situations that tempt you to light up – such as stress, boredom, a low mood, anxiety and worries, coffee, meals and pubs – can help you find other ways to enhance your sense of control and find new meaningful activities. Mindfulness (page 63) and active relaxation (page 113) may help you tackle smoking triggered by anxiety or depression. In addition, a few other tips may make life easier.

- Set a quit date. Smokers are more likely to quit if they set a specific date rather than saying, for example, that they will give up in the next two months.

- Quit abruptly. People who cut back the number of cigarettes they smoke usually inhale more deeply to get the same amount of nicotine. Nevertheless, cutting back makes it more likely that you will eventually quit by up to 70 per cent. Reduction takes you a step towards kicking the habit – but don't stop there.
- Smoking is expensive. Keep a note of how much you save and spend at least some of it on something for yourself.
- Ask if your area provides NHS anti-smoking clinics, which offer advice, support and, when appropriate, NRT (see <www.nhs.uk/smokefree/help-and-advice/local-support-services-helplines> for further information). Smokers in England can also obtain support from the free Smokefree National Helpline (0300 123 1044). In Wales, contact 0800 085 2219 (<www.helpmequit.wales>), in Scotland call 0800 84 84 84 (<www.nhsinform.scot/care-support-and-rights/nhs-services/helplines/quit-your-way-scotland>) and check out <www.want2stop.info> in Northern Ireland.
- Hypnosis (page 110) can increase the chances of quitting smoking almost five-fold according to an analysis of four studies.[113] Contact the British Association of Medical Hypnosis.

Dealing with setbacks

Nicotine is incredibly addictive. So, most smokers make three or four attempts to quit before they succeed.[18] Regard any relapse as a temporary setback, set another quit date, try again and try to identify why you relapsed. Were you stressed out, anxious or depressed? Did a particular time, place or event cause you to light up? Once you know why you slipped you can develop strategies to stop the problem. As the old health promotion advertisement suggests, 'do not give up on giving up'.

Drinking

Alcohol abuse is not confined to homeless drunks or 'partying' weekenders sprawled senseless. According to the Health and Social Care Information Centre (now NHS Digital), in 2014, 58 per cent of people over 16 years of age in Great Britain drank alcohol in the previous week – that's some 28.9 million people. Indeed, 2.5 million people drank more than 14 units on their heaviest drinking day. Like smokers, drinkers gamble with their health. Heavy drinking increases the risk of about 40 ailments, including cirrhosis (scarring of the liver), some cancers, strokes, heart disease, as well as injury or death from drowning, fires and other accidents.

Alcohol abuse, anxiety and depression

As mentioned before, alcohol abuse is common in people with anxiety and depression, as the following examples illustrate.

- Almost a fifth (18 per cent) of people with GAD (page 26) use alcohol to alleviate anxiety.[115]
- A Dutch study found that people currently experiencing depression or anxiety were almost three times more likely to develop alcohol dependence for the first time. Recent negative life events also increased the likelihood of alcohol dependence.[125]
- Researchers divided people in five groups based on the severity of their anxiety and depression. Two per cent of those with the mildest anxiety and depression had a recurrence of their alcohol dependence over the next two years. This rose to 15–29 per cent and 22–25 per cent of those in the two most severe groups for depression and anxiety respectively.[126]

Several factors link alcohol with anxiety and depression. For example:

- alcohol misuse often disrupts family and social life, causes employment and legal difficulties, and damages health, which can lead to or exacerbate depression;
- alcohol misuse and depression can arise from the same cause – some people may, for example, become depressed and drink excessively after they lose their job;
- as we have seen, some people drink as self-medication to drown the sorrows caused by depression;
- alcohol abuse may reduce levels of folate (page 76) and disrupt sleep (page 120), both of which can increase the risk of depression.

In addition, genetic factors that predispose to depression may only come to the fore in people who usually cope when these people drink excessively. Furthermore, around 50 to 60 per cent of the risk of developing alcoholic liver disease or becoming addicted to drink depends on your genes.[127]

Going it alone

Despite the harm caused by alcohol, despite alcohol abuse being largely outside the person's control, and despite addicts needing help, a review of 28 studies concluded that health professionals generally had negative attitudes towards people that abused alcohol or illicit drugs. In turn, professionals' negative attitudes reduced patients' feelings of empowerment and undermined how well the treatment worked.[128] You may be lucky enough to have a sympathetic doctor. If not, you may have to go it alone or seek help from a support group or a therapist.

Am I drinking excessively?

The UK's Chief Medical Officers suggest that for men and women who drink regularly or frequently (in other words, most weeks), 'it is safest not to drink more than 14 units a week on a regular basis. If you regularly drink as many as 14 units per week, it is best to spread your drinking evenly over 3 or more days.' If you have a health problem, are taking medicines (including those for depression and anxiety) or are pregnant, you should follow your doctor's advice: your limit may differ from the government's recommendation. So, how can you tell if you are abusing alcohol? You may have an alcohol problem if you answer 'yes' to two or more of the following questions.

C: Have you ever felt you should cut down on your drinking?
A: Have people annoyed you by criticizing your drinking?
G: Have you ever felt bad or guilty about your drinking?
E: Have you ever had a drink first thing in the morning (an eye opener) to steady your nerves or to get rid of a hangover?

This 'CAGE questionnaire' is not perfect. The 'ever' phrase means that CAGE captures people who had a drink problem, but who now

A UK unit of alcohol

A UK unit of alcohol contains 8 grams alcohol. So, one unit is:

- half a pint of normal-strength beer, lager or cider;
- one small (100-millilitre) glass of wine;
- a single (25-millilitre) measure of spirits.

A large (175-millilitre) glass of wine equals two units, and one 275-millilitre bottle of alcopop (5.5 per cent by volume) equals 1.5 units.

   Some studies and websites refer to an American 'drink', which contains 14 grams of alcohol or just less than 2 British units.

abstain or drink safely. The Alcohol Use Disorders Identification Test (AUDIT) is more detailed (<https://patient.info/doctor/alcohol-use-disorders-identification-test-audit>). However, do not leave it too late: most people deny that they abuse alcohol until health, social or legal problems emerge.

Tips to cut down

Most people try to reduce their drinking themselves before seeing a doctor or joining a group such as Alcoholics Anonymous. The first step is to record, over a month or so, how much you drink and when – places, circumstances (e.g. social situations) and emotions (such as when you are depressed or anxious). For instance, walking past your local can trigger an urge for a pint, a meal in a favourite restaurant can trigger a desire for a bottle of wine. Keeping a diary can help you discover that your anxiety and depression are part of a hangover or arise from guilt after a binge. The diary may show that you might drink to alleviate your anxiety and depression. Both might contribute. Unless you keep a diary, you won't know. You need to note how much you drink and not just guess. You may find that keeping track means that you start cutting down.

If you get so drunk that you cannot recall how much you drank the night before, you almost certainly have a problem. Your drinking pattern offers another clue. Most people vary their drinking pattern. People who abuse alcohol tend to drink more regularly, in some people to stave off withdrawal symptoms. Typically, withdrawal symptoms peak between 24 and 48 hours after the last drink and include shakes, insomnia, seizures, agitation, anxiety and depression. Returning to your old pattern after abstaining is also common in people who abuse alcohol.

You should set a goal. (If you suffer from a serious physical disease, speak to your doctor). Some people who drink heavily will need to abstain, probably for the rest of their life. However, other people find that they can cut back and drink within the recommended limit. Nevertheless, they need to remain alert for changes in their drinking habits.

Even if you plan to return to drinking safe levels of alcohol, it is worth not drinking for at least a month to allow your body a chance to recover. (If you cannot stop drinking for a few weeks, you might have an alcohol problem.) Other people find that it is easier to gradually reduce the amount they drink. Use your diary to track your progress and avoid slips. As you dry out, consider taking a milk thistle (*Silybum marianum*) supplement, which helps the liver heal.

(You can learn more in my book *Coping with Liver Disease*, which looks at alcohol's harmful effects in detail.) Interestingly, traditional herbalists believe that milk thistle is an antidepressant.[129] Liver disease can, partly by letting ammonia and other toxins build up in the blood, cause depression and other mental problems. By helping the liver heal, milk thistle might tackle this cause of depression, which, I believe, might partly account for its traditional use as an antidepressant.

Deciding whether or not to tell people you are cutting down can be tough. Some family and friends may offer advice and support. Others may feel that you are challenging their drinking – and may prove hostile or condescending, especially if some of your social life or occupation revolves around drinking. In such cases, offer to be the designated driver or tell a white lie and claim that you are on medication and your doctor has advised you not to drink. In any case, people taking antidepressants and anxiolytics need to check with their doctor about how much they can safely drink. You

---

Tricks to cut back on drinking

Various tricks can help you reduce your alcohol consumption:

- replace large glasses with smaller ones;
- use a measure at home rather than guess how many units you're pouring;
- only drink alcohol with a meal;
- avoid wine with an alcohol by volume (ABV) of 14 per cent or 15 per cent. Buy wine that is 10 per cent ABV or less instead;
- alternate alcoholic and soft drinks;
- try drinking spritzers and shandies rather than wine and beer;
- quench your thirst with a soft drink rather than an alcoholic beverage;
- have several 'dry' (drink-free) days each week, which might mean avoiding your usual haunts and drinking partners on dry days;
- find a hobby that does not involve drinking;
- try to buy rounds only when you are in small groups, as groups buying rounds tend to keep pace with the fastest drinker;
- if you rely on a nightcap to get to sleep, try the tips on page 120;
- if you drink to drown your sorrows, stress, depression or anxiety, try the problem solving techniques (page 66), mindfulness (page 63) or active relaxation (page 113).

could say that your doctor advised you not to drink, then change the subject.

If you just cannot quit

Several books and websites can help you reduce your drinking. If you feel you really cannot quit without help, your doctor can refer you to NHS Alcohol Services or offer drugs to help you deal with cravings. Psychotherapy can help you understand why you drink, how to cut down and how to deal with difficult situations. Alcoholics Anonymous, other support groups and formal religious activities also help some people overcome alcohol abuse (page 89).

Excessive caffeine

Coffee and other caffeine-containing drinks are something of a double-edged sword for people with depression and anxiety. Regularly drinking coffee seems to help prevent depression, although the reasons for this are not clear. For example, in one study, middle-aged men who drank more than 813 millilitres of coffee a day (very roughly, 2–3 mugs) were 77 per cent less likely to develop depression than those who did not drink coffee, even after allowing for other lifestyle factors that can contribute to depression. Drinking tea had no effect on depression and caffeine itself did not seem to account for the link.[130]

At the same time, too much caffeine can lead to poor sleep, which often seems to precede depression.[131] A high intake of caffeine – perhaps over 250 milligrams, although this varies between people – may directly trigger panic attacks and exacerbate anxiety. A high intake leaves some people with headaches and feeling nervous, irritable and agitated. They may find that they breathe rapidly, feel shaky and their muscles may twitch.[12, 131, 132] Indeed, the symptoms of excessive caffeine intake can be indistinguishable from anxiety.[12] One patient with severe anxiety that was unrelieved by tranquillizers and other drugs drank about 50 cups of coffee a day.[12]

Our susceptibility to caffeine seems to vary markedly, partly based on how well you get rid of caffeine from the body and on the amount you normally consume. (You become tolerant to caffeine's effects – so you have to drink more to get the same effect.) Similarly, stopping the regular consumption of caffeine – even small amounts (about 100 milligrams) in sensitive people – can produce withdrawal symptoms. You may experience, for example, anxiety, low mood, nausea, vomiting and, most commonly, headaches and tiredness. Symptoms begin to emerge about 12 hours after the last drink and peak after one or two days' abstinence.[131]

So, how much is safe to drink? According to the NHS, pregnant women should consume no more than 200 milligrams of caffeine a day: too much caffeine increases the risk of low birth weight and miscarriage.[131] For the rest of us, up to about 400 milligrams of caffeine a day probably will not do any harm. As a rule of thumb, 4 or 5 cups of coffee contains about 400 milligrams of caffeine. However, in 2001, the Food Standards Agency analysed 400 samples of tea and coffee bought from cafés, shops and so on, or brewed at home or work. The amount of caffeine varied widely:

- tea contained, on average, 40 milligrams caffeine, but ranged from 1 to 90 milligrams;
- instant coffee contained, on average, 54 milligrams of caffeine, ranging from 21 to 120 milligrams;
- ground coffee contained, on average, 105 milligrams caffeine, ranging from 15 to 254 milligrams a serving.

You need to decide how much caffeine is right for you (Table 6.1). It's worth remembering, however, that high coffee and caffeine consumption tends to be associated with an unhealthy lifestyle.[133] For instance, a large can of energy drink can contain 50 to 60 grams – 12.5 to 15 teaspoons – of sugar.

Table 6.1 The amount of caffeine in common foods and drink

Food or drink	Caffeine content
Can or bottle of energy drink	30 to 500 milligrams
Mug of filter coffee	140 milligrams
Mug of instant coffee	100 milligrams
Mug of tea	75 milligrams
Bar (50 grams) of plain chocolate	Up to 50 milligrams
Can of cola	40 milligrams
Bar (50 grams) of milk chocolate	Up to 25 milligrams

Source Adapted from NHS Choices <www.nhs.uk>; Szpak and Allen[131]

Avoid dehydration

If you cut down on alcoholic and caffeinated drinks, you need to make sure you drink enough. Even the mild dehydration that might arise during our daily activities can cause unpleasant symptoms including:

- reduced vigilance and concentration;
- poor memory;
- fatigue;
- headache;
- and increased tension and anxiety.[134, 135]

The NHS suggests that adults should drink 1.2 litres (six to eight glasses of water) each day to replace fluids they lose in urine, sweat and so on. If you feel thirsty for long periods, you're not drinking enough. Increase your intake during exercise or hot weather, if you feel light-headed, pass dark-coloured urine or haven't passed urine within six hours. If you regularly feel thirsty despite maintaining your fluid intake, you should see your doctor. Excessive thirst can be a symptom of diabetes.

7

Get out and about

We did not evolve to live cheek-by-jowl, to be surrounded by glass and concrete, to rush around in cars, or spend hours crushed on public transport. For millennia we lived in forests, fields and fen. Instead of the roar of traffic, we knew the boom of a bittern, the bark of a vixen and the growl of a badger. Instead of being crushed together, we lived in open spaces.

Most of us – 80 per cent, the World Bank estimates – live in towns and cities. Yet despite our increasingly urban lifestyles, Richard Mabey comments, 'myths and symbols' of nature still pervade our culture. We use nature as a source of metaphors and emblems of 'decay and rebirth'. So, perhaps it's not surprising that for many people, getting back to nature alleviates depression and anxiety, and bolsters their stress defences. In *Nature Cure*, Richard Mabey movingly describes his recovery from severe depression after moving from the Chiltern Hills to Norfolk. It's an old idea: 'the healing currents of the outdoors' can rinse away ill health, he notes. In addition, a walk in nature gets us away from places that we associate with our mental distress. And, of course, a walk in the countryside is excellent exercise (page 99). However, nature's benefits come from more than exercise alone: they are psychological and spiritual as well.

Nature improves recovery from surgery

In a now famous study, Roger Ulrich from Delaware University in the USA compared recovery in two groups of patients who had undergone a common type of gall bladder surgery. One group could look out of a window at a small stand of deciduous trees. The other group could see only a brown, brick wall. The rooms were otherwise nearly identical and Ulrich allowed for other factors – such as age – that might influence recovery. For example, the same nurses looked after both groups of patients. For several years, Ulrich collected data about patients' recovery between May and October, when the trees had foliage.[136]

People who could see the trees spent, on average, just under a day less in hospital than those who looked at a brick wall. Nurses were also around four times less likely to make negative comments in the medical notes – such as 'upset and crying' or 'needs much encouragement' – and more likely to make positive observations – including 'in good spirits' and 'moving well' – about people who looked out on the trees.[136] Patients with a view of the trees were also slightly less likely to experience minor complications – such as nausea and headache – following their operation. The group facing the wall needed many more doses of potent painkillers (such as opioids) than those with a view of trees. In general, those able to look at the trees also used less potent painkillers, such as aspirin and paracetamol.[136] These findings suggest that the view of the trees boosted recovery, and reduced pain and stress. In other words, a view of nature produces measurable biological changes.

Forest bathing

Similarly, Japanese people believe that walking in forests promotes physical and mental health. The Japanese term *Shinrin-yoku* – forest bathing – means 'making contact with and taking in the atmosphere of the forest'.[137] Just looking at a picture of people walking in a forest reduces blood pressure, researchers found. However, the smell and other sensations of walking through a forest augment the visual appreciation.[138] As the East Anglian writer Ronald Blythe notes, in *From the Headlands*, when nature is 'right under our noses, we inhale it as well as comprehending it with our intellects'. You absorb the 'earthy patterns and colours . . . instinctively as well as intellectually'.

Certainly, exercise only accounts for some of the *Shinrin-yoku*'s benefits. For example, several studies compared people who walked or sat in forests to those who took a similar amount of exercise in towns and cities. The forest bathers produced less cortisol – a hormone released during stress – and showed lower blood pressure and pulse rates. Forest bathing also seems to boost immunity. Just walking in a forest for 15 minutes and then sitting for another 15 minutes enhanced feelings of vigour, while reducing depression, tension and anxiety compared to walking and sitting in an urban environment. The benefits were especially marked in people who felt chronic mental stress.[138]

So, make the most of the more than 400 country parks and many other nature reserves in England alone. The following websites are good places to start for information:

- Natural England <www.gov.uk/government/organisations/natural -england>
- The National Trust <www.nationaltrust.org.uk>
- Ramblers <www.ramblers.org.uk/go-walking.aspx>
- The Royal Society for the Protection of Birds <www.rspb.org.uk/ reserves>
- The Woodland Trust <www.woodlandtrust.org.uk>.

Why exercise helps

Part, but not all, of nature's benefits come from the regular exercise. Indeed, anxiety and depression are about half as common in people who exercise as their more sedentary counterparts.[21] For example, resistance exercises (such as weight training and press-ups) increase strength, skeletal muscle mass, endurance and power – and seem to help alleviate depression and anxiety. In one article, researchers combined the results of 33 studies and found that resistance exercises reduced depressive symptoms. Indeed, on average, symptoms declined by almost half (45 per cent) from those experienced before the exercise sessions began.[207]

People who exercise regularly are less likely to develop panic disorder, agoraphobia, social phobia, GAD or specific phobias.[3] Exercise also seems to enhance recovery. In one study, 47 per cent of people taking antidepressants recovered from their depression during a four-month study. Rather than taking antidepressants, researchers asked other people to exercise three times a week: a 10-minute warm up, followed by walking or jogging for 3 minutes, then a 5-minute cool down. About 45 per cent of those who researchers supervised on a treadmill in a gym and 40 per cent of those who researchers asked to follow the same regimen at home recovered. In contrast, only 31 per cent of those taking a placebo recovered.[139]

People with anxiety are particularly sensitive to changes in their body, especially those they associate with anxiety or a panic attack. Exercise produces many of the same changes – such as an increased heart rate, sweating and breathlessness. In other words, exercise allows you to become used to the sensations. As they become familiar, they are less likely to trigger anxiety or panic attacks. In one study, for example, high-intensity exercise reduced anxiety more effectively than low-intensity workouts. This probably reflects the more marked internal changes produced by intensive exercise.[3] In some cases, anxiety sensitivity can change after working out for only two weeks – about six 20-minute sessions. The improvement was broadly similar to that after three months – twelve 90-minute sessions – of psychotherapy.[21]

Exercise also seems to enhance the person's feeling that they can cope and are self-efficient. In other words, exercise helps engender an 'internal locus of control' (page 13). Indeed, some people find that certain exercises are especially effective at fostering self-efficiency. In one study, 45 minutes of martial arts reduced anxiety and improved mood more than the same time on an exercise bicycle. In another study, people who took part in three hour-long yoga sessions (page 112) a week for 12 weeks showed greater improvements in anxiety, tranquillity and 'revitalization' than those who burnt the same calories off walking.[3]

Getting enough exercise

In addition to the psychological benefits, exercise increases mobility, strength and stamina, and helps protect against osteoporosis (weak, easily broken bones), hypertension, heart attacks, strokes and so on. Exercise also helps you control your weight. To gain these benefits, you should be moderately active for at least 30 minutes on at least five days – and ideally every day – a week. It does not all have to be in one go. You can exercise for 15 minutes twice a day, for example. You should feel that your heart is beating faster than usual and you have begun to sweat. The talking test is one way to tell. If you can talk, but not sing, you are probably working out at a moderate level.[21] However, if you experience chest pain or feel faint or otherwise unwell, stop exercising and see your doctor.

Exercise as part of everyday life

You should aim to make exercise part of your everyday life. If you stop after exercising regularly for a year, you will lose about half your cardiovascular fitness in three months. So, find a type of exercise that you enjoy and that fits into your lifestyle. If you do not like exercise classes and you join a gym some distance from home or work, you are more likely to quit. On the other hand, you can easily integrate walking or, in some parts of the country, riding a bike into your daily life.

Social physique anxiety – anxiety about other people evaluating your appearance – can act as a barrier to exercise[3] if, for example, you have social anxiety or are overweight. You might be better off with a solitary activity – walking, jogging or using an exercise bike at home – at least until you get your confidence back. And set realistic expectations.[21] It doesn't matter how long I work out, I will never model for *GQ*. Yet some people still have unrealistic expectations of what exercise can offer.

As we've seen, people with anxiety or depression tend to withdraw socially and become inactive. These 'maladaptive' coping strategies help perpetuate the anxiety and depression. Exercise requires action and, often, engagement with other people.[3] So, team sports help some people with anxiety and depression. For example, feedback from teammates can challenge feelings of inadequacy and inferiority and counter isolation.[21] Obviously, choose your sport and teammates carefully. Some spectators and teammates seem to revel in 'trash talking' – even during 'friendly' weekend games.

Find a time of day to exercise that suits you. Some people find that exercising in the morning helps them focus better on the day.[21] That's fine if you can jog or cycle to work and can have a shower when you arrive. However, some people simply cannot get up early enough (their body clock is more attuned to the evenings that the mornings), have a long commute, have to use dangerous roads, or need to get the kids to school. They would probably be better off exercising in the evening. Nevertheless, there are plenty of other opportunities to make exercise part of your day-to-day life.

- Clean the house regularly and wash your car by hand.
- Grow your own vegetables (they taste better as well).
- If you take the bus, tube or metro, get off one or two stops early.
- Park a 15-minute walk from your place of work.
- Use the stairs instead of the lift.
- Walk to the local shops instead of taking the car.

Finally, don't delay – although if you have a serious physical health problem check with your doctor – and protect the time in your diary. You may find it difficult to exercise because you do not consider working out to be as important compared to other demands.[21] It's like leaving work until close to a deadline: you forget about the other demands and distractions that might emerge. So, don't delay exercise – or any other lifestyle change until life is less demanding. You'll probably be just as busy as you are now.

Spirituality and religion

Nature acts on more than our physical and emotional sides. Intense experiences evoked by nature – as well as music, and even some sciences – can create 'self-transcendent wonder' that's akin to spirituality.[140] Indeed, spirituality is part of being human. More than 40,000 years ago, Neanderthal and Palaeolithic man engaged in complex religious rituals, seemed to 'understand' the idea of death, and drew images of mythical creatures on cave walls.[141] As Polkinghorne points out: 'at almost all times and in almost all places, human beings have participated in an admittedly bafflingly diverse history of encounters with the sacred'.[142]

Religion and spirituality overlap – but are not identical. Some people see religion as a 'social' or 'cultural' obligation and attend religious services regularly. However, they are decidedly unspiritual. Some deeply spiritual people do not follow a 'recognized' religion.

Religion and spirituality bolster your defences

Whatever path you follow, religion and spirituality bolster your defences against stress and, therefore, depression and anxiety, as the examples below show.

- Religious people with depression show greater purpose, optimism, generosity and gratefulness.[143] These characteristics aid recovery from a bout of depression.
- In Jewish adolescents, being religious reduced self-harmful thoughts and behaviours by 55 per cent, even after allowing for depression, social and economic factors.[144]
- People at low risk of depression who attended religious services at least once a month were about 83 per cent less likely to have an episode of major depression during the next 10 years.[145]
- Most people – between 77 and 83 per cent of adults aged at least 55 years – preferred therapies for anxiety and depression that included religion, spirituality or both. People who thought that including religion or spirituality in therapy was important reported more positive religious-based coping, and greater collaborative and less self-directed problem solving than those who did not think it was important.[146] Indeed, depressed and anxious people who received CBT that included religion showed a more rapid improvement than with conventional CBT, although the long-term benefits were broadly similar.[147]

Spot the difference

Differentiating religion and spirituality taxes theologians. Essentially, however, religion refers to a group's collective spiritual experiences based around organized beliefs and practices. Spirituality covers a much wider range of beliefs, experiences and values than any one religion. Sheldrake comments that, broadly, spirituality refers to 'lifestyles and practices that embody a vision of human existence and of how the human spirit is to achieve its full potential'. Spirituality is 'holistic . . . A fully integrated approach to life',[140] encompassing personal practices and attitudes that typically:

- foster and promote 'connections' with yourself and others;
- include a search for life's meaning and purpose;
- offer a cohesive system of values, usually encompassing love (in the broadest sense), compassion and justice.

Spirituality is a personal search, alone or in a group. Some people follow a single path – as with an organized religion. Other people 'pick' from a spiritual smorgasbord, choosing elements from various traditions. This diversity means that everyone can probably find a set of spiritual values that 'works for them'. Many followers of conventional religions criticize this trend towards 'pick and mix' spirituality. Whether or not they're right, the variety makes studying spirituality's effect on mental and physical health notoriously difficult. Three people – a pagan, a Zen Buddhist and a Sikh – may all be deeply spiritual. But isolating the influence of their lifestyles, personality and psychology from the impact of their spirituality is almost impossible.

To try to reduce the confusion, many investigations study organized religions, which at least have a consistent core of beliefs. However, the benefits offered by most organized religions extend beyond the spiritual. For example, organized religions offer a sense of community and friendship, practical support and a structured lifestyle (such as bans on drugs and alcohol). Spiritual leaders, for instance, are often fonts of wisdom as well as practical and emotional support. Such factors might help account for some of the benefits on health and well-being in general, and for people with anxiety and depression in particular. But teasing out spirituality's benefits is difficult.

Religions may also bolster the effectiveness of conventional medicine. Some religions engender a 'respect' for authority, which increases the chances that people will follow their doctor's advice. Indeed, people who report higher levels of spiritual well-being are more likely to take their medicine as their doctors suggest.[148] As people may need to take antidepressants and anxiolytics for several months or even years and psychotherapy requires commitment, adherence is important and may influence the link between health, religion and spirituality.

Religion's ability to bolster defences against stress, depression and anxiety is probably one reason why religious people are less likely to become addicted to drink and drugs than their more secular counterparts.[149] In an English study, religious people were 27 per cent less likely to have used drugs and 19 per cent less likely to drink heavily than those who were neither religious nor spiritual.[149]

Furthermore, former problem drinkers who integrate religious and spiritual activities into their daily life are more likely to remain sober than those who did not, even after allowing for participation in Alcoholics Anonymous. Private religious and spiritual practices (such as prayer and reading spiritual texts) and forgiving themselves (most drinkers suffer profound guilt about the harm they have done to themselves and others) were especially effective. In fact, including spirituality in former drinkers' daily lives predicted their chance of long-term sobriety more strongly than their levels of stress or contentment.[150] In many ways, the 12-step programme used by, among others, Alcoholics Anonymous 'encourage[s] a personal belief system based on spiritual self-discovery'.[140]

Many people abuse drink or drugs to help them 'cope' with depression, anxiety, PTSD or other emotional or mental problems. When they stop their substance abuse, the void remains – and, in many cases, the addiction has deepened the emotional and psychological chasm. So, they switch to another addiction to fill the gap, such as overeating, compulsive shopping or excessive exercise. Religious and spiritual practices help fill the void and reduce the risk that they will swap one addiction for another.

Side effects of religion and spirituality

However, it's not all good news. In a study from England, spiritual people were found to be more likely to have abnormal eating attitudes (by 46 per cent), GAD (50 per cent) or a phobia (72 per cent). Spiritual people were also found to be 40 per cent more likely to be taking a medicine for a psychiatric illness.[149] Some people turn to religion and spirituality as solace in times of stress, which might partly account for the link. In addition, some religious people also hold unrealistically high expectations for themselves and others, which can lead to isolation, stress and anxiety. In other cases, members of a religious community may isolate themselves from other people who do not share their beliefs[151] or feel – or are told – that their suffering is God's punishment, both of which can exacerbate or trigger anxiety and depression.

You can even have too much faith. An American study found that people who used religious coping mechanisms following a heart attack were more likely to experience depression while in hospital and over the following month. Some people seem to 'over-rely' on their relationship with God to aid their recovery, which can develop into a form of fatalism.[152] The lack of drive and motivation common in people with anxiety and depression can enhance fatalism. Recovering from anxiety and depression depends on taking an active approach to care: God helps those who help themselves.

Social networks

Religion and many spiritual pathways create a sense of community and belonging, which can bolster your mental and physical health. In one group of people at high risk of depression, good social adjustment reduced the risk of an episode by about 80 per cent.[145] Close family and friends and a strong marriage (which means any type of 'life partnership') can offer social, practical and emotional support to help you cope with stress and recover from anxiety and depression. Indeed, people with strong social connections show less marked changes in blood pressure when they face high levels of negative emotions than those with fewer or weaker networks.[153] (Raised blood pressure is part of the 'natural stress response'). On the other hand, married women who lack intimacy and have no close relationships outside the house are prone to depression.[15]

Your partner's and family's practical and emotional support can be invaluable if you are trying to drink less alcohol, quit smoking, take more exercise, change your diet or stick with psychotherapy, antidepressants or anxiolytics. For example, your partner can help you adopt a healthy lifestyle, ignore bad moods triggered by an illness or lifestyle change, boost your motivation when you feel like quitting and watch for harmful behaviours. But some family members and friends – especially if they have expressed concerns about your drinking, eating, smoking and so on – might not be as understanding if you slip back: it is easy to underestimate how difficult changing your lifestyle can be, especially if you have depression and anxiety. So, as mentioned above, think carefully before you tell family and friends.

In other words, the quality of your social networks matters as much as, if not more than, the quantity: you need to develop relationships that preserve or enhance your emotional well-being and bolster your ability to cope[153] and disengage from relationships that are counterproductive. After all, social networks that encourage drug abuse, heavy drinking or cause profound stress are hardly good for your mental or physical health. In some cases, such as your family, you may not be able to remove yourself from the network. However, you can probably find ways to limit their influence. (Again, counselling might help you deal with counterproductive relationships.)

Meanwhile, partners need to tread the fine line between 'nagging' (even with the best intentions) and 'support'. A spouse's *support* – helping and reinforcing their loved one's efforts to tackle unhealthy behaviours – improved the mental health of people after a heart attack or by-pass surgery. However, *control* – trying to persuade a partner to adopt healthy behaviours when he or she is unwilling or unable – reduced the likelihood that the person would make the changes and undermined mental health.[154]

A menagerie of therapeutic animals

For centuries, healers have used a menagerie of animals – including dogs, cats, guinea pigs, rabbits and horses – to bolster well-being. Disabled people in Belgium helped care for farm animals in the ninth century. In the 1700s, the York Retreat – which was well ahead of its time – used rabbits, seagulls, hawks and other domestic animals to promote well-being in people with mental illness. Florence Nightingale suggested that a small pet 'is often an excellent companion' for ill people, especially those with chronic conditions.[155]

Animals help people with depression and anxiety in several ways. First, for example, animals offer uncritical companionship. Their care can create a purpose in life and evoke pleasant memories, which helps 'distract' people from a problem or their depression and anxiety. Some people speak more openly to their pet than their spouse, probably because animals are, obviously, non-judgemental – and this helps get problems off the owner's chest. As one of George Eliot's characters remarks: 'Animals are such agreeable friends – they ask no questions, pass no criticisms'.

Walking the dog can help prevent people from becoming housebound, and offers a sense of security. This can help counter agoraphobia and withdrawal. Walking the dog is also great exercise, which helps counter depression and anxiety. Caring for, and interacting with, animals alleviates stress and reduces blood pressure, heart rate and cholesterol levels. Even a fish tank in a dentist's waiting room reduces anxiety in what many people find an intensely stressful situation.[155] In other words, religion, spirituality and human and animal companionship are powerful means to tackle depression and anxiety.

8

Active relaxation and complementary therapies

Many people with depression and anxiety seek solace in alternative and complementary therapies. Complementary therapies do not replace mainstream medicines. Rather, complementary therapies help control symptoms, improve well-being, enhance quality of life and augment the efficacy of conventional drugs and psychotherapy. However, never stop a medicine or reduce a drug's dose without speaking to your doctor first. Unfortunately, we can only skim the surface of this vast area – numerous books cover the various options. If you want to try a complementary therapy, check with your doctor first if you have a long-standing physical illness. Then consult a registered practitioner, such as one recognized by the General Regulatory Council for Complementary Therapies or the Complementary and Natural Healthcare Council. Read up on the approach you are planning to use and make sure you understand the risks and benefits.

Once therapy begins, watch for side effects. For example, some alternative healers believe that complementary therapies drive out toxins – such as mercury, lead and other heavy metals – that have accumulated in your body and contribute to your depression and anxiety. Some alternative therapists say that this toxic 'tsunami' can produce a detox 'crisis', characterized by unpleasant symptoms including headaches, fatigue and abdominal discomfort. In some cases, the healer and patient undergoing detox can dismiss adverse events as a crisis. So, be careful if you experience unexpected symptoms.

Courting controversy

Despite being popular and despite millions of people feeling they benefit from them, complementary medicines often attract considerable controversy, in part because traditional explanations fit uneasily with modern medicine. For example, a paper in the prestigious *Archives of Internal Medicine* that considered 31 studies, which included almost 18,000 people, reported that acupuncture roughly halved the intensity of chronic pain caused by back, neck and shoulder problems, osteoarthritis and headache.[156] (Chronic pain commonly causes depression and anxiety.) Few conventional, western doctors accept the traditional Chinese explanation that acupuncture balances the flow of *chi* (life force) along 12 meridians (channels) linking our organs and systems. Yet, the paper points out, 'there is no accepted mechanism by which [acupuncture] could have persisting effects on chronic pain'.[156]

Similarly, no accepted mechanism explains acupuncture's benefits in depression. In a study from the north of England, the severity of moderate to severe depression halved in 33 per cent of patients treated with an average of ten sessions of acupuncture compared to 29 per cent with an average of nine sessions of counselling, and 18 per cent with usual care. On average, people treated with acupuncture had 34 days free from depression over three months, compared to 27 days with counselling and 23 days with usual care. Essentially, acupuncture was as effective after three months and a year as counselling, and both were better than usual care despite 76 per cent of the people having experienced at least four previous episodes of depression. Further studies need to define the most effective course of treatment and the people most likely to respond.[157]

Cynics often point to the lack of evidence supporting many complementary therapies – acupuncture and certain herbs are notable exceptions. Certainly, few complementary therapies undergo the same rigorous testing as modern medicines. However, clinical trials are expensive and usually funded by pharmaceutical companies. So, this lack of evidence isn't surprising. Indeed, as we have seen, the scientific evidence for medicines is not always definitive (page 36). No evidence of effectiveness is not necessarily the same as evidence of no effect.

To complicate matters further, complementary therapists often combine approaches. For instance, naturopathic healers treated 41 people who experienced moderate to severe anxiety with dietary advice, deep breathing relaxation, a standard multi-vitamin, and the Ayurvedic herbal medicine ashwagandha (*Withania somnifera*), also called Indian ginseng. Another 40 people received psychotherapy, performed deep breathing relaxation techniques and placebos for the herbs and vitamins. After 12 weeks, anxiety scores declined by approximately 57 per cent with naturopathic care and 31 per cent in those treated with psychotherapy. Naturopathic care also alleviated fatigue and improved mental health, concentration, social functioning, vitality and overall quality of life.[158] However, identifying which element or elements were responsible is difficult, especially as the effects may be additive or synergistic.

Cynics tend to dismiss complementary medicine's success as 'just a placebo effect'. Yet, as we have seen, the placebo response contributes to every conventional medicine, every psychotherapy session, every complementary therapy. So, keep a diary noting symptoms and triggers. You may feel initially better from the placebo effect, but this usually wanes. If you don't feel any benefit after three months, discuss whether it is worth continuing.

Types of complementary medicine

Broadly, complementary medicines fall into one of four types.[159]

1 Mind–body practices integrate the brain, mind, body and behaviour. Such practices include deep breathing, meditation, yoga, progressive muscle relaxation, t'ai chi, qi gong, hypnosis and biofeedback.
2 Natural products, including herbs, vitamins, minerals and other supplements, such as omega-3 fatty acids (page 78). Naturopathy and aromatherapy also use natural products. In one study, for example, the aroma of sweet orange reduced anxiety.[160]
3 Manipulative and body-based practices – such as massage, Alexander technique, shiatsu, chiropractic and osteopathy – that focus on bones, joints, muscles, and so on.
4 A mixed bag of other therapies, including energy field manipulation (e.g. crystal therapy, reiki, therapeutic touch) and whole medicine systems, such as traditional Chinese, Arabic (Unani) and Ayurvedic medicines, homeopathy and naturopathy.

In other words, there is a vast range of complementary treatments, with widely differing levels of evidence and 'plausibility', at least according to conventional western medicine. Mainstream doctors usually dismiss some therapies – such as reflexology, crystal therapy and reiki – out of hand. In other cases, it's hard to see the boundary between mainstream and complementary medicines. Ayurvedic is a mainstream medicine in India. However, most conventional doctors in the UK regard Ayurvedic medicine as complementary.[18]

Given this choice, it is important to take advice from your doctor or patient group and read up on the approach you want to try. In this section, we'll look at some approaches, supported by studies, that illustrate the potential offered by complementary therapies.

However, this list is not exhaustive and you should find the approach that works for you.

Biofeedback

Biofeedback allows you to exert some control over the 'autonomic' nervous system, which maintains essential functions without conscious control. The autonomic nervous system, for example, keeps us breathing and our heart pumping while we're asleep. Biofeedback machines and software typically make a sound or show a display that monitors your heartbeat, brain waves, muscle tension, for example. By listening to the sounds or watching the display, practitioners train themselves to regulate the signals and, in turn, heartbeat, blood pressure, respiration, muscle tension and so on. Some biofeedback experts suggest that the approach is especially effective for somatic (physical) symptoms (page 8). Biofeedback may convert the somatic symptoms back into emotions. This helps raise awareness of the underlying distress, feelings and conflicts.[47]

There's strong scientific evidence that biofeedback helps several conditions, including anxiety, attention, chronic pain, constipation, headache, hypertension and motion sickness.[159] Several commercial biofeedback machines and computer programs are available, which you can use alongside other approaches such as deep breathing (page 112), progressive muscular relaxation (page 113), mindfulness (page 63) and meditation (page 65). You may need to practise biofeedback regularly (e.g. twice a day for 20 minutes) and periodically reinforce your technique.[47]

Hypnosis

For centuries, conventional doctors dismissed hypnotism as a stage trick, with any benefits confined to weak-willed, gullible people – usually women or those of lower social status than the doctors. In 1890, the *British Medical Journal* called hypnotism 'a dangerous mental poison, and as such it needs to be fenced round with as many restrictions as the traffic in other kinds of poison'. The *British Medical Journal* added that hypnotism is 'fraught with many dangers to the nervous equilibrium and psychological soundness of the subject'.[161]

Some doctors suggested that subjects 'faked' responses to please their hypnotist. Yet in 1829, the French doctor Pierre-Jean Chapelain used hypnosis as an anaesthetic during a mastectomy for breast cancer.[113] Then in 1842, a 'respectable' surgeon from Nottingham used hypnotism during an operation to amputate a patient's leg. At the time, patients often needed to be drunk and tied down during an operation. Around the same time, James Esdaile, a Scottish surgeon working near Calcutta, removed a scrotal tumour using hypnosis as anaesthesia.[162] It is hard to believe someone would endure the pain of a mastectomy, amputation or scrotal operation to please the surgeon. Modern powerful painkillers and anaesthetics meant that healers no longer resort to hypnosis. Nevertheless, these examples underscore hypnotism's power. Today, doctors still do not fully understand how hypnotism works. Essentially, however, hypnosis is focused attention and concentration. Some hypnotists describe the process as similar to being 'so lost in a book or movie that it is easy to lose track of what is going on around you'.[113]

Despite Victorian doctors' cynicism – who probably worried that hypnotism could take some of their business – hypnosis helps control pain, alleviate stress and change harmful habits, such as abusing alcohol, comfort eating or smoking. Hypnosis is safe: a hypnotist cannot make you do or say anything he or she wants. You will be able to come 'out' of hypnosis whenever you want.[113] You could also try self-hypnosis. Numerous DVDs, CDs and books help you create the 'focused attention' that underpins hypnosis. Contact the British Association of Medical Hypnosis for further information.

T'ai chi and qi gong

Meditation doesn't always mean sitting in the lotus position chanting 'om' or another mantra. T'ai chi, qi gong, yoga and rosary prayer are all forms of meditation. However, learning classical meditation can be difficult without guidance. Many local adult education centres hold courses. Your vicar or spiritual adviser can educate you about the best way to pray.

T'ai chi (*t'ai chi ch'uan*) is a 'soft' or 'internal' martial art combining deep breathing, meditation and relaxation with sequences (called forms) of slow gentle movements that enhance fitness, strength and flexibility. So, t'ai chi is often suitable (after checking with your doctor) for people with chronic physical diseases, such as chronic obstructive pulmonary disease (COPD), Parkinson's disease and arthritis. The increased movement helps counter the depression and anxiety left in the wake of a chronic illness. Like any martial art, t'ai chi can bolster confidence, foster self-efficiency and help develop an internal locus of control (page 13). As we've seen, these benefits are especially useful for people trying to overcome anxiety and depression.

T'ai chi may look undemanding until you try it. Learning the t'ai chi short form takes about 12 lessons, but many years to master. Speeded up, t'ai chi can offer effective self-defence: *ch'uan* means 'fist'. Speed up a raising hand and you may deflect a blow to the head, while a descending hand can deflect a kick. Contact the Tai Chi Union for Great Britain.

Qi gong also combines deep breathing, meditation, relaxation and movements. However, the movements are more internally focused on the 'flow of energy' around the body than in t'ai chi.[159] Nevertheless, some practitioners regard t'ai chi as a form of qi gong.[47] *Qi* (also pronounced chi) is the life energy. *Gong* means training, work or cultivation. According to qi gong practitioners, the movements help gather energy and cultivate the spirit and, in turn, protect against stress, depression and anxiety. Again, qi gong is often suitable for people who are recovering from illness, even if bedridden or in wheelchairs.[47] But check with your doctor. Contact the British Health Qigong Association or Health Qigong Federation UK.

Yoga

Yoga brings millions of people – from all religious backgrounds – inner peace, relief from stress and improved health. Yoga aims to harmonize consciousness, mind, energy and body, by focusing on achieving controlled, slow, deep breaths, while the poses (asanas) increase fitness, strength and flexibility. As a result, yoga helps maintain suppleness of body and mind (some poses require considerable concentration). Clinical studies suggest that yoga may help people with, for instance, headaches, back and neck pain, fibromyalgia, depression and anxiety.[163,164] Indeed, yoga improves mood and reduces anxiety more than the same time spent walking.[165] Scientists are beginning to uncover the biological basis for yoga's benefits. For example, yoga lowers levels of cortisol, glucose, adrenaline and noradrenaline, which, we have seen, are biological messages intimately involved in the stress response. Yoga also reduces heart rate, blood pressure and inflammation, as well as boosting parts of our immune defences.[166] Contact the British Wheel of Yoga for more information.

Think about your breathing

One of the first things a yoga, martial arts or meditation teacher will probably tell you is that you are not breathing correctly. Breathing correctly can produce marked physical effects. For example, changes in the number of breaths you take can alter your heart rate by 12 to 15 beats per minute. As you breathe more deeply, more oxygen reaches your blood and your heart does not need to work as hard. The brain detects the increase in oxygen and nerves tell the heart that it does not need to pump as hard. This 'feedback' between mind and body means you don't feel mentally stressed when your body is relaxed and vice versa.

On the other hand, breathlessness commonly triggers anxiety and panic attacks. Unfortunately, becoming anxious exacerbates breathlessness. Breathing too quickly can bring on anxiety by lowering the amount of carbon dioxide in your lungs. This can arise from slightly over-breathing for a long time and so, does not have to be obvious. Sometimes even a yawn or sigh triggers a panic attack or anxiety's physical symptoms.

Most of us breathe shallowly, using the upper parts of our lungs. Try putting one hand on your chest and the other on your abdomen. Then breathe normally. Most people find that the hand on their chest moves while the one on their abdomen remains relatively still. To fill your lungs fully, try to make the hand on your abdomen rise, while keeping the one on the chest as still as possible. Breathing deeply and slowly without gasping helps relaxation. You can also try changing your breathing pattern as a first aid for stress:

- breathe in deeply through your nose for a count of four;
- hold your breath for a count of seven;
- breathe out for a count of eight;
- repeat a dozen times.

Active relaxation

There is nothing wrong with curling up with a good book or watching your favourite television programme or movie. However, many of us need to take a more 'active' approach to relaxation. NICE notes, for example, that relaxation therapies – including progressive muscle relaxation (PMR), meditation, yoga, assertiveness training and anger control techniques – reduce blood pressure by around 3.5 mmHg. A third of people using these techniques show at least a 10 mmHg reduction in blood pressure – a similar improvement as that produced by many drugs for hypertension. In other words, active relaxation produces measurable biological benefits.

Finding time to relax

The following tips should help you relax your mind and body. You may need to adapt these suggestions if, for example, you want to meditate or practise yoga.

- Try to follow your 'active relaxation' therapy every day. Many people find early morning best. The house is quiet and you will be better able to focus and less likely to drop off to sleep than at night.
- Make yourself comfortable in a chair that supports your back or lie down. You might want to put cushions under your neck and knees. Take off your shoes, switch off any bright lights and ensure the room is neither too hot nor too cold.
- Shut your eyes and, if it helps, play some relaxing music and burn some aromatherapy oils or incense formulated to aid relaxation.

Do not try to perform relaxation therapy on a full stomach. After a meal, blood diverts from your muscles to your stomach. For example, trying PMR on a full stomach can cause cramps. Relaxation can make you more aware of your body's functions. A full stomach can be a distraction.

Progressive muscular relaxation

PMR aims to relax each part of your body in turn. Try putting your hands by your side, then:

- clench your fists as hard as you can and hold the fist for ten seconds;
- slowly relax your fist and let your hands hang loosely by your sides;
- shrug your shoulders as high as you can, then hold for ten seconds and relax slowly;
- gently arch your back, hold for ten seconds and relax;
- tense your muscles as you inhale;
- while you are tense, try to breathe slowly and rhythmically;
- exhale as you relax.

Repeat each exercise three times, slowly, gently and gradually.

PMR teachers usually advise mastering one muscle group at a time. So, it could take two or three months before you can tense and relax your entire body.

We become used to a certain amount of muscle tension as we go about our daily lives. Our necks feel stiff. Our jaw muscles clench.

We frown. Everyone does – but muscle tension is often especially marked in people with depression or anxiety. With practice, the awareness of your body engendered by PMR helps you to recognize when your muscles are tense. You can then use PMR to relax the tense muscles. But if you suffer from back problems, arthritis or another serious medical condition or ailment, check with your doctor before trying PMR.

Herbalism

Herbalism is one of the longest established medical traditions, perhaps even dating from before we became recognizably *Homo sapiens*. Chimpanzees and gorillas, for example, deliberately 'self-medicate' with plants active against parasites, often using the same herbs as local human healers.[167] In 1960, archaeologists discovered a Neanderthal skeleton buried in caves in Shanidar, Iraq, surrounded by several plants used by modern herbalists – including cornflower, yarrow and ground-sel. Some archaeologists believe the plants probably formed part of the Neanderthals' pharmacy. Today, herbal and other treatments remain important. According to the World Health Organization, 80 per cent of the population in some Asian and African countries depend on traditional medicine for their health care.

When tradition trumps technology

Sometimes traditional medicine seems to owe more to superstition than to science. However, traditional frameworks – even astrological correspondences, such as linking Mercury and Saturn with melancholia – allowed healers to recognize patterns, organize knowledge and apply collective wisdom to particular problems.[162] Patients often benefited from this collective wisdom. Malaria, for instance, was the scourge of Europeans visiting the tropics. In the early seventeenth century, explorers in South America learned that the bark of the cinchona tree alleviated malarial fevers. We now know that a chemical in the bark – quinine – kills the parasite that causes malaria, but at the time, physicians believed that a benevolent God placed cures for an area's afflictions in the local environment – such as dock leaves near stinging nettles.

In 1763, the chaplain Edward Stone found that willow bark alleviated ague, a fever caused by malaria, which was then rife in England. Aspirin is a chemically modified, less toxic version of the active ingredient in willow bark. Again, willow grows near the water that can harbour mosquitoes that transmit malaria. Whether you organize your knowledge based on a belief in a benevolent God, a chemical's biological benefits, or both, cinchona and willow still work.

Over the years, healers have tried numerous remedies for depression and anxiety including:

- bog myrtle, chervil and nettle for low mood;[47]
- passion flower, skull cap, chamomile and hops, which are mild sedatives, 'calmatives' and may aid with sleep disturbances;[47]
- valerian, a common herbal remedy for insomnia, 'calms' the mind and may alleviate anxiety.[129]

Some traditional remedies stack up well against modern medicines. For instance, scientific studies show that kava kava and St John's wort are as effective as conventional medicines for many cases of anxiety and depression. Furthermore, some sleep and 'stress' supplements available from supermarkets and pharmacists contain herbs such as hops, valerian, passion flower and chamomile. In one study, high-quality (so-called pharmaceutical grade) chamomile extract (1,500 milligrams a day) for up to eight weeks produced a 'clinically meaningful' improvement in the symptoms of moderate to severe GAD. Indeed, the response rate was, the authors comment, similar to that produced by conventional anxiolytics. No one developed serious side effects.[197]

St John's wort

St John's wort (*Hypericum perforatum*), a small yellow flower on a plant that grows up to a metre high, is as effective as conventional anti-depressants for mild to moderate depression, including seasonal affective disorder. Some medical herbalists suggest taking an extract for mild anxiety. You may also see St John's wort mixed with other herbs including lemon balm and hops for people who experience problems sleeping.

Like all plants, St John's wort is a complex, complicated mix of chemicals. One chemical – called hyperforin – is an antibiotic. Another chemical, called hypericin, is responsible for its antidepressant actions and may act, at least in part, as an SSRI. In a Cochrane review of 29 trials, between 28 per cent and 87 per cent of people with depression, depending on the way the study was designed (page 36), responded to hypericum extracts. Indeed, extracts of St John's wort were, broadly, as effective as tricyclic antidepressants and SSRIs. For instance, one study compared 12 weeks of treatment with a standardised extract of St John's wort, fluoxetine (Prozac) or a placebo. Symptom scores were lower among people with depression taking St John's wort than with fluoxetine or the placebo. Furthermore, 38 per cent of those taking St John's wort entered remission compared with 30 per cent with fluoxetine and 21 per cent with the placebo.

More recently, researchers reviewed 27 clinical trials during which 3,808 people with mild to moderate depression received either St John's wort or an SSRI. St John's wort and SSRIs produced similar outcomes in terms of the number of patients in whom symptoms improved and who went into remission. People taking St John's wort were, however, 41 per cent less likely to stop treatment (for example, because of side effects) than those taking SSRIs. The studies lasted between 4 and 12 weeks, however, and further studies are needed to fully characterize the relative benefits in the long term. Additional studies, the researchers suggest, should determine whether or not St John's wort helps people with severe depression.[198]

St John's wort also seems to produce fewer side effects than standard antidepressants.[168] In the Cochrane review, 76 per cent fewer people with depression stopped taking St John's wort compared to older antidepressants, such as tricylics. Furthermore, 47 per cent fewer people stopped St John's wort compared to SSRIs.

You can buy St John's wort – often marked as hypericum – as tablets, capsules, a tea and a tincture, which you take as drops added to water. The formulation isn't standardised in the UK. So, you need to read the label carefully. According to MIND, a typical dose is between 200 mg and 1000 mg of a 0.3 per cent standardised hypericum extract. Always follow the label or, even better, see a medical herbalist especially, as St John's wort can cause side effects (including sedation and an increased chance of sunburn)[15] and interact with other drugs and herbs. For example, when combined with other drugs that affect levels of serotonin, St John's wort can trigger the serotonin syndrome.[169] In addition, St John's wort can cause potentially dangerous interactions with, for example, benzodiazepines, warfarin, statins, verapamil, digoxin and oral contraceptives.[170] If you are in any doubt, speak to your doctor or pharmacist and it's probably prudent to seek advice from a medical herbalist.

The serotonin syndrome

The serotonin syndrome, caused by dangerously high levels of the neurotransmitter, is potentially life threatening. See a doctor urgently if you are taking antidepressants and experience any of these symptoms: confusion, agitation, overactive reflexes, profuse sweating, shivering or tremor, nausea, diarrhoea, lack of coordination, fever, coma, flushing, or swollen and painful muscles.[169]

Kava kava

Kava kava *(Piper methysticum)* derives its name from the Polynesian word *awa*, meaning bitter. Traditional preparations made from the shrub produce mild intoxication and are central to many ceremonial and social gatherings in Pacific Island culture.[171] Some researchers believe that kava kava's relaxant and calming effects may help account for the low risk of alcohol misuse in the traditional societies across Polynesia, Melanesia and Micronesia that use the herb.[52] Traditional healers also used kava kava to treat diseases including gonorrhoea, syphilis, cystitis and insomnia.[171]

In Europe, historically, herbalists used kava kava to treat anxiety, nervousness and tension[52] – and clinical trials suggest that it works.[171] For example, after six weeks' treatment, 26 per cent of people with GAD taking kava kava extract had entered remission. This compared to 6 per cent of those taking a placebo. Anxiety scores at least halved in 37 per cent of those taking kava kava, compared to 23 per cent who received the placebo.[172] In a German study, 56 per cent of people with GAD taking kava kava extract were 'much' or 'very much' improved and, after 8 weeks, 37 per cent seemed to be in remission. The effect was broadly similar to two conventional drugs used to treat GAD in Germany. There wasn't a placebo arm. However, based on previous studies, kava kava's effect is 25 per cent greater than a placebo, which is again broadly similar to the benefit produced by conventional drugs.[52] Several other studies confirm these findings.[52] Herbalists also report that kava kava promotes a restful sleep without the loss of mental clarity,[47] which can occur with some tranquillizers and sleeping pills.

Nevertheless, kava kava can cause serious side effects such as skin redness, headache and liver damage.[171,172] Indeed, by 2006, the Food Standards Agency had received 110 reports over several years in which kava kava possibly caused liver damage. Eleven patients received liver transplants and nine died. **Kava kava sales are now banned in the UK.** However, you may come across kava kava on the internet and mentioned in self-help books. (You must be careful buying any medicine, including herbs and supplements, on the internet. Always use a reputable site.)

Ginseng

Ginseng *(Panax ginseng* and *Panax quinquefolius)* seems to produce a variety of health benefits including: boosting the immune system; reducing inflammation; mopping up tissue-damaging free radicals; and countering excessive stress. Asian cultures value ginseng as a way to boost energy. Moreover, ginseng might modulate neurotransmitters and encourage growth of new nerve cells.[86] As mentioned above (page 17), people with depression can show decreases in the size of certain areas of the brain.

Ginseng may be a potentially valuable addition to conventional antidepressants. In one study, women who experienced residual symptoms (page 49) while in remission on antidepressants took 3 grams of ginseng a day for eight weeks. Their residual psychological and somatic symptoms improved. Side effects included gastrointestinal disturbances, headache and sleep changes. Studies using a placebo need to confirm these promising findings[86] and ginseng can interact with some medications – so always check. (As an aside, other herbs likely to interact with conventional medicines include liquorice, ginkgo and schisandra.[71]) However, you might want to consider ginseng if you experience residual symptoms or feel you need a energy boost.

A complex mix

Studying herbs' benefits, side effects and interactions can prove difficult: plants contain a mixture of chemicals, several of which can contribute to the benefits and adverse events. To complicate matters further, many herbal formulations contain several plants: some traditional Chinese medicines include more than 20 components. On the other hand, the amount of biologically active chemicals in a herb is less than that in a conventional medicine. While this means that you are less likely to experience side effects, the benefits can take longer to emerge or may not be as marked. Nevertheless, if you develop any signs or symptoms that could be side effects, stop taking the formulation and see your medical herbalist. If you fail to see any benefits after three months, you should think about stopping the herb.

If you decide to try herbal remedies or other supplements, make sure you buy reputable preparations from a shop with knowledgeable staff. You should also look for standardized extracts: the amount of active ingredient can vary depending on where it is grown and when it is harvested. (That may be one reason why some traditional herbals suggest gathering the plant at a particular time or associate the herb with a particular astrological sign.) Before you embark on a course of herbal supplements, speak to your pharmacist, doctor or medical herbalist. Not all products include the detailed information you need in order to take the supplement safely. Indeed, it is best to consult a qualified medical herbalist and make sure to tell him or her about any conditions you have and any conventional medicines you are taking.

A good night's sleep

Sleep problems are among the most common, most distressing and most debilitating of all the constellation of symptoms linked to anxiety and depression. About 70 to 90 per cent of depressed people report sleep-related problems, including difficulty falling asleep, frequent awakenings, early morning waking and daytime tiredness. Indeed, for some people depression is, predominantly, a disorder of sleep rather than mood.[173] Moreover, lack of sleep can trigger an episode of depression as well as making you feel tense, anxious and nervous. Indeed, shift workers seem to be particularly prone to developing depression.[177] Some antidepressants (such as the tricyclics) are sedatives in people without depression. At least some of their benefits might reflect their effect on sleep rather than depression itself.[199] So, try our tips for a good night's sleep. If these do not work, you could try one of the herbal treatments or medicines from your pharmacist for sleep disturbances or see your doctor. However, even herbal remedies are short-term, rather than long-term, solutions.

Tips for a good night's sleep

- Wind down or relax at the end of the day: do not go to bed while your mind is racing, ruminating or pondering problems.
- Try not to take your troubles to bed with you. Brooding makes problems seem worse, exacerbates stress, keeps you awake and, because you are tired in the morning, means you are less able to deal with your difficulties. Try to avoid anxiety-provoking conversations and arguments before bed.
- Do not worry about anything you have forgotten to do. Get up and jot it down (keep a notepad by the bed if you find you do this a lot). This should help you forget about the problem until the morning.
- Go to bed at the same time each night and set your alarm for the same time each morning, even at the weekends. This helps re-establish a regular sleep pattern.
- Avoid naps during the day.
- Avoid stimulants, such as caffeine and nicotine, for several hours before bed. Try hot milk or milky drinks instead.
- Do not drink too much fluid (even non-alcoholic) just before bed as this can mean regular trips to the bathroom.
- Avoid alcohol. A nightcap can help you fall asleep. However, as blood alcohol levels fall, sleep becomes more fragmented and lighter. So, you may wake repeatedly in the latter part of the night.

- Do not eat a heavy meal before bedtime. Ideally, eat at the same time each day and try to finish the last meal of the day at least three hours before you plan to go to bed.[177]
- Although regular exercise helps you sleep, exercising just before bed can disrupt sleep. Try not to exercise in the four hours before you plan to go to bed.[177]
- Use the bed for sex and sleep only. Do not work, watch TV or use computers or smart phones. Minimize light exposure for at least 30 minutes before you plan to go to sleep.[177]
- Make the bed and bedroom as comfortable as possible. Invest in a comfortable bed, mattress and pillows, use enough bedclothes, and make sure the room is not too hot, too cold or too bright.
- If you cannot sleep, get up and do something else. Watch the TV or read – nothing too stimulating – until you feel tired. Lying there worrying about not sleeping keeps you awake.
- Create a bedtime routine that you find relaxing, such as reading or listening to music.[177]

Taking laughter seriously

You can literally die laughing. Strong emotions, even when positive, can increase the risk of suffering a heart attack and stroke. More commonly, however, laughter is a great healer. As the great seventeenth-century English physician Thomas Sydenham remarked,

Laughter's biological benefits

Initially, laughter and tears increase levels of adrenaline and noradrenaline in the blood, which, in turn, speeds heart rate and elevates blood pressure. A relaxation phase follows – which is why you may feel 'pleasantly drained' after laughing or crying.[92] Laughter produces a range of biological benefits including:

- bolstering immune defences;
- decreasing levels of stress hormones;
- enhancing memory, creative thinking, problem solving and so on;
- exercising and relaxing muscles;
- improving respiration, especially by promoting deep breathing (page 112);
- increasing the pain threshold and tolerance;
- stimulating blood circulation.

'the arrival of a single clown has a more healthful impact on the health of a village than that of 20 asses laden with medications'.

So, why does laughter help? Freudian psychoanalysts (page 57) believe that humour 'distances' us from problems, places issues in perspective, reframes problems, minimizes distress and releases tension.[174] Laughter fosters a constructive mental outlook that counters stress, depression, insomnia and loneliness, and enhances self-esteem, hope, mood, energy and vigour.[92,175] Laughter and tears may also reduce the 'social and emotional distance between people', which, in turn, helps generate compassion, encourages human contact and resolves interpersonal conflicts.[92] In other words, humour and tears can help bridge the gap between people – acting as an intuitive interpersonal therapy. As we've seen, this gap contributes to some cases of anxiety and depression. Indeed, laughter possibly evolved as a signal of safety and security to other people.[174] The benefits are so marked that some hospitals and hospices run laughter and humour sessions – including visits from clowns – teach laughter meditation or run laughter clubs.[174] You could also curl up with a comedy DVD, CD or book. You may be able to have the last laugh over your depression or anxiety.

Summing up

The American Psychological Association have proposed several ways to help build resilience to depression and anxiety, which won't be a surprise after reading this book. (I have adapted these in line with the rest of the book. You can find the original here: <www.apa.org/ Helpcenter/road-resilience.aspx>.)

1 *Make connections and relations* A network of supportive relationships with family, friends, voluntary groups, religious organizations and charities helps protect against stress, depression and anxiety. Many people find that helping others helps them, partly by taking their minds off their depression and anxiety. Do not be afraid to express your emotions or talk about your problems with friends, family or a professional. Try to accept help and support from other people. 'Pulling yourself' out of depression or anxiety is difficult and, for some people, impossible. We need all the help we can get.

2 *Acknowledge that you can overcome your problems* You can overcome your depression and anxiety. You can resolve or come to terms with the underlying problems and issues. You cannot alter events in the past and you may not be able to change the future. Remember, even if you cannot change your circumstances, you can alter your reaction. Psychotherapy can nurture your internal

locus of control, an important weapon in the fight against depression and anxiety, and help you develop effective and efficient coping strategies.

3 *Accept that everything changes* The Greek philosopher Heraclitus famously commented, about 2,500 years ago, 'Everything changes, nothing stays still . . . You cannot step into the same stream twice'. You may need to accept that circumstances mean you can no longer attain a once-treasured ambition or keep a relationship or job. Depression commonly develops in people in their 40s,[12] a time when many people realize that they will not reach their youthful goals or when children start becoming independent. Falling short of our aspirations and ambitions, and our children growing up, can cause stress, anxiety and depression. So, accept that some circumstances cannot be changed and rethink your goals.

4 *Develop and move towards realistic goals* Try to take small steps – every day if you can, even if it is a relatively minor advance – that takes you closer to your goal. Begin by identifying your problems and finding solutions. Then devise a plan, broken into short-term goals.

5 *Do not be passive* Withdrawing excessively or hoping your problems will sort themselves out (a type of denial) are common coping strategies, but they can make your anxiety and depression worse. Instead, identify your problems and take action. Being proactive engenders an internal locus of control, one of the best defences against anxiety and depression.

6 *Make the most of the problem* Addressing the issues that cause anxiety and depression means embarking on a voyage of discovery about yourself, your circumstances, your work and social networks. At times, you may enter choppy waters. But if you stay on course and address the underlying issues and your unhelpful behaviours – for example, by psychotherapy – you may emerge from a bout of depression or anxiety with a sense of inner strength, self-worth, spirituality and a heightened appreciation for life.

7 *Keep your problems in perspective* Try to take a broad view of your life, relationships and circumstances. Try to count your blessings; some people even make a list. It's all too easy, when you are in the midst of depression or anxiety, to lose track of the things that are going well. Try to avoid making mountains out of molehills, which, as we've seen, is a hallmark of some types of anxiety. You could ask yourself whether the problem will still be an issue in six months' or a year's time. Humour, literature and the other arts, visiting museums, walking in nature can all help create and maintain a sense of perspective.

8 *Look after yourself* What do you need to do to help yourself cope? Find the time to take part in activities that you enjoy. You may need to find the time to take a more active approach to relaxation and to exercise. Stick to a routine: regular sleep, quit smoking, not drinking too much caffeine or alcohol, taking exercise and finding time for spirituality.

9 *Find other ways to bolster your inner resources* Keep a diary, meditate or invest more time in your spiritual or religious practices. You may decide to join an organized religious group, which can offer practical and social as well as spiritual support. Indeed, many religious leaders are excellent counsellors. Alternatively, try local classes in yoga, meditation, t'ai chi or mindfulness.

10 *Stay positive and nurture hope and optimism* As you address your anxiety and depression, you'll develop confidence in your ability to solve problems and learn to trust your instincts. An active approach to tackling problems can help. Success breeds success. Moving towards your goal boosts confidence, bolsters your internal locus of control and helps tackle stress. This, in turn, helps reduce the chance that your anxiety and depression will recur.

11 *Do not forget about the healing power of humour* Optimism and hope aid recovery from depression and anxiety, and bolster your defences against stress, which also helps reduce the risk of another episode. Try focusing on your goals, rather than ruminating on your current problems – see if mindfulness or meditation helps.

Tackling anxiety and depression can be extremely difficult – especially as medicines are, at best, only part of the answer. You might not be able to get psychotherapy quickly on the NHS. You might find the cause of the problems lies buried under the experiences of numerous difficult years or in a tangled web of relationships. Anxiety and depression can feel like prison sentences. However, you can break free. I wish you well.

Useful addresses

Action on Smoking and Health
Sixth Floor, Suites 59–63
New House, 67–68 Hatton Garden
London EC1N 8JY
Tel.: 020 7404 0242
Website: www.ash.org.uk

Alcohol Concern
27 Swinton Street
London WC1X 9NW
Tel.: 020 3907 8480
Website: www.alcoholconcern.org.uk

Alcoholics Anonymous
PO Box 1
10 Toft Green
York YO1 7NJ
Tel.: 0800 9177 650 (national helpline)
Website: www.alcoholics-anonymous.org.uk

Alliance of Suicide Prevention Charities
Website: www.tasc-uk.org

Anxiety Alliance
26 Tannery Court
Bertie Road
Kenilworth
Warwickshire CV8 1QY
Tel.: 0845 296 7877 (helpline: 10 a.m. to 10 p.m., 7 days a week)
Website: www.anxietyalliance.org.uk

Anxiety UK
Zion Community Centre
339 Stretford Road
Hulme
Manchester M15 4ZY
Tel.: 03444 775 774 (helpline: 9.30 a.m. to 5.30 p.m., Monday to Friday)
Website: www.anxietyuk.org.uk

Breathing Space
Tel.: 0800 838587 (helpline: 6 p.m. to 2 a.m., Monday to Thursday; 6 p.m. Friday to 6 a.m. Monday)
Website: http://breathingspace.scot

British Association for Behavioural and Cognitive Psychotherapies
Imperial House
Hornby Street
Bury
Lancashire BL9 5BN
Tel.: 0161 705 4304
Website: www.babcp.com

British Association for Counselling and Psychotherapy
BACP House
15 St John's Business Park
Lutterworth
Leicestershire LE17 4HB
Tel.: 01455 883300
Website: www.bacp.co.uk

British Association of Medical Hypnosis
45 Hyde Park Square
London W2 2JT
Tel.: 07711 681134
Website: http://bamh.org.uk

British Dietetic Association
Fifth Floor, Charles House
148/9 Great Charles Street Queensway
Birmingham B3 3HT
Tel.: 0121 200 8080
Website: www.bda.uk.com
Listing of Freelance Dieticians: https://freelancedietician.org

British Health Qigong Association
Website: http://healthqigong.org.uk

British Psychoanalytic Council
Suite 7, 19–23 Wedmore Street
London N19 4RU
Tel.: 020 7561 9240
Website: www.bpc.org.uk

British Psychoanalytical Society
The Institute of Psychoanalysis
Byron House
112a Shirland Road
London W9 2BT
Tel.: 020 7563 5000
Website: www.psychoanalysis.org.uk

British Psychological Society
St Andrews House
48 Princess Road East
Leicester LE1 7DR
Tel.: 0116 254 9568
Website: www.bps.org.uk

British Psychotherapy Foundation
37 Mapesbury Road
London NW2 4HJ
Tel.: 020 8452 9823
Website: www.britishpsychotherapyfoundation.org.uk

British Thyroid Foundation
Suite 12, One Sceptre House
Hornbeam Square North
Hornbeam Park
Harrogate HG2 8BP
Tel.: 01423 810093
Website: www.btf-thyroid.org

British Wheel of Yoga
25 Jermyn Street
Sleaford
Lincolnshire NG34 7RU
Tel.: 01529 306851
Website: www.bwy.org.uk

C.A.L.L. Helpline (Community Advice and Listening Line Wales)
Tel.: 0800 132 737 (24 hours a day, 7 days a week)
Website: http://callhelpline.org.uk

Campaign Against Living Miserably (male suicide prevention)
PO Box 68766
London SE1P 4JZ
Tel.: 0800 585858 (national helpline); 0808 802 5858 (London helpline);
(both helplines: 5 p.m. to midnight, 365 days a year)
Website: www.thecalmzone.net

Centre for Mental Health
Tel.: 020 7717 1558
Website: www.centreformentalhealth.org.uk

Child Bereavement UK
Clare Charity Centre
Wycombe Road
Saunderton
Buckinghamshire HP14 4BF
Tel.: 01494 568900; 0800 02 888 40 (helpline: 9 a.m. to 5 p.m., Monday to Friday)
Website: https://childbereavementuk.org

Choose Life (Suicide Prevention in Scotland)
Website: www.chooselife.net

Combat Stress (the Veterans' Mental Health Charity)
Tyrwhitt House
Oaklawn Road
Leatherhead
Surrey KT22 0BX
Tel.: 0800 138 1619 (helpline)
Website: www.combatstress.org.uk

Complementary and Natural Healthcare Council
Albert Buildings
49 Queen Victoria Street
London EC4N 4SA
Tel.: 020 3668 0406
Website: www.cnhc.org.uk

The Confederation of Healing Organisations (and British Register of Complementary Practitioners)
Coombedene
Coombe Hill
Keinton Mandeville
Somerton
Somerset TA11 6DY
Tel.: 0300 302 0715
Website: http://icnm.org.uk

COSCA (Counselling and Psychotherapy in Scotland)
16 Melville Terrace
Stirling FK8 2NE
Tel.: 01786 475140
Website: http://cosca.org.uk

Cruse Bereavement Care
PO Box 800
Richmond
Surrey TW9 1RG
Tel.: 0808 808 1677 (helpline)
Website: www.cruse.org.uk

Depression UK
PO BOX 10566
Nottingham NG13 8LU
Website: http://depressionuk.org

General Regulatory Council for Complementary Therapies
Box 437, Office 6
Slington House
Rankine Road
Basingstoke RG24 8PH
Tel.: 0870 314 4031
Website: www.grcct.org

Health and Care Professions Council
Park House
184 Kennington Park Road
London SE11 4BU
Tel.: 0300 500 6184
Website: www.hpc-uk.org

Health Qigong Federation UK
32 High Street
Chislehurst
Kent BR7 5AQ
Website: www.healthqigong.co.uk

HOPELine UK
Tel.: 0800 068 41 41 (helpline: 10 a.m. to 10 p.m., weekdays; 2 p.m. to
5 p.m., weekends and Bank Holidays)
Website: https://papyrus-uk.org/help-advice/about_hopelineuk

Mental Health Foundation
Colechurch House
1 London Bridge Walk
London SE1 2SX
Tel.: 020 7803 1100
Website: www.mentalhealth.org.uk

Mental Health Research UK
Robertson Pugh & Co.
3 Leicester Road
Oadby
Leicester LE2 5BD
Website: www.mentalhealthresearch.org.uk

Mental Health Wales (Hafal)
Unit B3
Lakeside Technology Park
Phoenix Way
Llansamlet
Swansea SA7 9FE
Tel.: 01792 816600
Website: www.mentalhealthwales.net

MIND
15–19 Broadway
Stratford
London E15 4BQ
Tel.: 020 8519 2122
Website: www.mind.org.uk

OCD-UK
Marble Hall (Office 5)
80 Nightingale Road
Derby DE24 8BF
Tel.: 03332 127 890
Website: www.ocduk.org

PANDAS Foundation (Pre- and Postnatal Depression Advice and Support)
The Fort
Artillery Business Park
Park Hill
Oswestry SY11 4AD
Tel.: 0843 28 98 401 (helpline: 9 a.m. to 8 p.m., 7 days a week)
Website: www.pandasfoundation.org.uk

Papyrus (Prevention of Young Suicide)
Lineva House
28–32 Milner Street
Warrington
Cheshire WA5 1AD
Tel.: 01925 572 444 (helpline: 0800 068 41 41)
Website: https://papyrus-uk.org

Phobics Society
Website: www.phobics-society.org.uk

Rethink Mental Illness
89 Albert Embankment
London SE1 7TP
Tel.: 0121 522 7007 (general enquiries); 0300 5000 927 (helpline:
9:30 a.m. to 4 p.m., Monday to Friday)
Website: www.rethink.org

Samaritans
The Upper Mill
Kingston Road
Ewell
Surrey KT17 2AF
Tel.: 116 123 (helpline: 24 hours a day, 365 days a year)
Website: www.samaritans.org

SANE
St Mark's Studios
14 Chillingworth Road
Islington
London N7 8QJ
Tel.: 020 3805 1790; 0300 304 7000 (helpline: 4.30 p.m. to 10.30 p.m.,
365 days a year)
Website: www.sane.org.uk

Scottish Association for Mental Health
Brunswick House
51 Wilson Street
Glasgow G1 1UZ
Tel.: 0141 530 1000
Website: www.samh.org.uk

Seasonal Affective Disorder Association
PO Box 332
Wallingford OX10 1EP
Website: www.sada.org.uk

Stroke Association
Stroke Association House
240 City Road
London EC1V 2PR
Tel.: 020 7566 0300; 0303 3033 100 (helpline: 9 a.m. to 5 p.m., Monday, Thursday and Friday; 8 a.m. to 6 p.m., Tuesday and Wednesday; 10 a.m. to 1 p.m., Saturday)
Website: www.stroke.org.uk

Survivors Trust (rape and sexual abuse)
Unit 2, Eastlands Court Business Centre
St Peter's Road
Rugby
Warwickshire CV21 3QP
Tel.: 01788 550554; 0808 801 0818 (helpline: 10 a.m. to 4 p.m. and 6 p.m. to 8 p.m. Monday to Thursday; 10 a.m. to 4 p.m. Friday)
Website: www.thesurvivorstrust.org

Tai Chi Union for Great Britain
Aileen Mandić (Cromar)
62a Greenock Road
Bishopton
Renfrewshire PA7 5JB
Tel.: 07802 705011
Website: www.taichiunion.com

Thyroid UK
32 Darcy Road
St Osyth
Clacton on Sea
Essex CO16 8QF
Tel.: 01255 820407
Website: www.thyroiduk.org.uk

Together
12 Old Street
London EC1V 9BE
Tel.: 020 7780 7300
Website: www.together-uk.org

Triumph Over Phobia (TOP UK)
PO Box 3760
Bath BA2 3WY
Tel.: 01225 571740
Website: www.topuk.org

Young Minds
Tel.: 020 7089 5050; 0808 802 5544 (helpline for parents and carers:
9.30 a.m. to 4 p.m., Monday to Friday)
Website: https://youngminds.org.uk

References

1 Cuijpers P. Bibliotherapy in unipolar depression: A meta-analysis. *Journal of Behavior Therapy and Experimental Psychiatry* 1997;28:139–47.

2 Haug TT, Mykletun A, Dahl AA. The association between anxiety, depression, and somatic symptoms in a large population: The HUNT-II study. *Psychosomatic Medicine* 2004;66:845–51.

3 DeBoer LB, Powers MB, Utschig AC, et al. Exploring exercise as an avenue for the treatment of anxiety disorders. *Expert Review of Neurotherapeutics* 2012;12:1011–22.

4 Holmes EA, Craske MG, Graybiel AM. Psychological treatments: A call for mental-health science. *Nature* 2014;511:287–9.

5 DeRubeis RJ, Hollon SD, Amsterdam JD, et al. Cognitive therapy vs medications in the treatment of moderate to severe depression. *Archives of General Psychiatry* 2005;62:409–16.

6 Kirsch I. *The Emperor's New Drugs: Exploding the Antidepressant Myth.* Bodley Head, 2009.

7 Read J, Cartwright C, Gibson K. Adverse emotional and interpersonal effects reported by 1829 New Zealanders while taking antidepressants. *Psychiatry Research* 2014;216:67–73.

8 McManus S, Bebbington P, Jenkins R, Brugha T (eds) *Mental health and wellbeing in England: Adult Psychiatric Morbidity Survey.* Leeds: NHS Digital, 2016. Available at <digital.nhs.uk/catalogue/PUB21748> [accessed January 2018].

9 Hoge EA, Ivkovic A, Fricchione GL. Generalized anxiety disorder: Diagnosis and treatment. *BMJ* 2012;345:e7500.

10 Andrews G, Poulton R, Skoog I. Lifetime risk of depression: Restricted to a minority or waiting for most? *The British Journal of Psychiatry* 2005;187:495–6.

11 Spijker J, de Graaf R, Bijl R, et al. Duration of major depressive episodes in the general population: Results from The Netherlands Mental Health Survey and Incidence Study (NEMESIS). *The British Journal of Psychiatry* 2002;181:208–13.

12 Iversen SD. *Pyschopharmacology: Recent Advances and Future Prospects.* Oxford University Press, 1985.

13 Nanni V, Uher R, Danese A. Childhood maltreatment predicts unfavorable course of illness and treatment outcome in depression: A meta-analysis. *The American Journal of Psychiatry* 2012;169:141–51.

14 Barbui C, Cipriani A, Patel V, et al. Efficacy of antidepressants and benzodiazepines in minor depression: Systematic review and meta-analysis. *The British Journal of Psychiatry* 2011;198:11–6.

15 Edwards V. *Depression: What You Really Need to Know.* London: Robinson, 2003.

16 Lasserre AM, Glaus J, Vandeleur CL, et al. Depression with atypical features and increase in obesity, body mass index, waist circumference, and fat mass: A prospective, population-based study. *JAMA Psychiatry* 2014;71:880–888.

17 Tylee A, Gandhi P. The importance of somatic symptoms in depression in primary care. *Prim Care Companion J Clin Psychiatry* 2005;7:167–76.

18 Russell A. *The Social Basis of Medicine*, first edition. Wiley-Blackwell, 2009.

19 Vallance A. Something out of nothing: The placebo effect. *Advances in Psychiatric Treatment* 2006;12:287–96.

20 Showalter E. *Hystories: Hysterical Epidemics and Modern Culture.* Picador, 1998.

21 Otto M, Smits J. *Exercise for Mood and Anxiety: Proven Strategies for Overcoming Depression and Enhancing Well-Being.* Oxford University Press, 2011.

22 Rojo-Moreno L, Livianos-Aldana L, Cervera-Martínez G, Dominguez-Carabantes JA, Reig-Cebrian MJ. The role of stress in the onset of depressive disorders. *Soc Psychiatry Psychiatr Epidemiol* 2002;37:592–8.

23 Renzaho AMN, Houng B, Oldroyd J, et al. Stressful life events and the onset of chronic diseases among Australian adults: Findings from a longitudinal survey. *European Journal of Public Health* 2014;24:57–62.

24 Bianchi R, Schonfeld IS, Laurent E. Is burnout a depressive disorder? A reexamination with special focus on atypical depression. *International Journal of Stress Management* 2014;21:307–24.

25 Meltzer H, Bebbington P, Brugha T, et al. The relationship between personal debt and specific common mental disorders. *The European Journal of Public Health* 2013;23:108–13.

26 Pizzagalli DA, Bogdan R, Ratner KG, Jahn AL. Increased perceived stress is associated with blunted hedonic capacity: Potential implications for depression research. *Behaviour Research and Therapy* 2007;45:2742–53.

27 Stansfeld S, Candy B. Psychosocial work environment and mental health – a meta-analytic review. *Scandinavian Journal of Work, Environment & Health* 2006;32:443–62.

28 Waugh CE, Koster EHW. A resilience framework for promoting stable remission from depression. *Clinical Psychology Review* 2014. DOI:10.1016/j.cpr.2014.05.004.

29 Uher R. Gene-environment interactions in severe mental illness. *Frontiers in Psychiatry* 2014;5:48.

30 Fabbri C, Porcelli S, Serretti A. From pharmacogenetics to pharmacogenomics: The way toward the personalization of antidepressant treatment. *Can J Psychiatry* 2014;59:62–75.

31 Annunziato A. DNA packaging: Nucleosomes and chromatin. *Nature Education* 2008;1:26. Available at: <www.nature.com/scitable/topic page/dna-packaging-nucleosomes-and-chromatin-310> [accessed June 2018].

32 Shipman P. Why is human childbirth so painful? *American Scientist* 2013;101:426–9.

33 Dowben JS, Grant JS, Keltner NL. Ketamine as an alternative treatment for treatment-resistant depression. *Perspectives in Psychiatric Care* 2013;49:2–4.

34 Duman RS, Aghajanian GK. Synaptic dysfunction in depression: Potential therapeutic targets. *Science* 2012;338:68–72.

35 Moncrieff J, Cohen D. Do antidepressants cure or create abnormal brain states? *PLoS medicine* 2006;3:e240.

36 Frasure-Smith N, Lespérance F, Talajic M. Depression follow-ing myocardial infarction: Impact on 6-month survival. *JAMA* 1993;270:1819–25.

37 Gupta S. Mental health: Ups and downs. *Nature* 2014;510:S10–S11.

38 Penninx BW, Milaneschi Y, Lamers F, Vogelzangs N. Understanding the somatic consequences of depression: Biological mechanisms and the role of depression symptom profile. *BMC Medicine* 2013;11:129.

39 Mezuk B, Eaton WW, Albrecht S, Golden SH. Depression and type 2 diabetes over the lifespan: A meta-analysis. *Diabetes Care* 2008;31:2383–90.

40 Luppino FS, de Wit LM, Bouvy PF, et al. Overweight, obesity, and depression: A systematic review and meta-analysis of longitudinal studies. *Archives of General Psychiatry* 2010;67:220–9.

41 Meng L, Chen D, Yang Y, et al. Depression increases the risk of hyper-tension incidence: A meta-analysis of prospective cohort studies. *Journal of Hypertension* 2012;30:842–51.

42 Postuma RB, Aarsland D, Barone P, et al. Identifying prodromal Parkinson's disease: Pre-motor disorders in Parkinson's disease. *Movement Disorders: Official Journal of the Movement Disorder Society* 2012;27:617–26.

43 Greener M. Tackling the burden of pain. *Nurse Prescribing* 2009;7:398–402.

44 Antonuccio D, Healy D. Relabeling the medications we call anti-depressants. *Scientifica* 2012;2012:965908.

45 Greener M. Beneath the surface: Dermatology and psychiatry. *Progress in Neurology and Psychiatry* 2014;18:16–8.

46 Snorrason I, Stein DJ, Woods DW. Classification of excoriation (skin picking) disorder: Current status and future directions. *Acta Psychiatrica Scandinavica* 2013;128:406–7.

47 Strohecker J, Strohecker N, Bresler D, editors. *Natural Healing for Depression*. Perigee Books, 1999.

48 Uutela A. Economic crisis and mental health. *Current Opinion in Psychiatry* 2010;23:127–30.

49 Bleakley S, Davies SJC. The pharmacological management of anxiety disorders. *Progress in Neurology and Psychiatry* 2014;18:27–32.

50 Thibodeau MA, Welch PG, Sareen J, Asmundson GJ. Anxiety disorders are independently associated with suicide ideation and attempts: Propensity score matching in two epidemiological samples. *Depression and Anxiety* 2013;30:947–54.

51 Allgulander C. Generalized anxiety disorder: A review of recent find-ings. *Journal of Experimental & Clinical Medicine* 2012;4:88–91.

52 Boerner RJ, Sommer H, Berger W, et al. Kava-Kava extract LI 150 is as effective as opipramol and buspirone in generalised anxiety disorder – An 8-week randomized, double-blind multi-centre clinical trial in 129 out-patients. *Phytomedicine* 2003;10:38–49.

53 Asselmann E, Wittchen H-U, Lieb R, et al. Associations of fearful spells and panic attacks with incident anxiety, depressive, and sub-stance use disorders: A 10-year prospective-longitudinal community study of adolescents and young adults. *Journal of Psychiatric Research* 2014;55:8–14.

54 Harvey SB, Hatch SL, Jones M, et al. The long-term consequences of military deployment: A 5-year cohort study of United Kingdom reservists deployed to Iraq in 2003. *American Journal of Epidemiology* 2012;176:1177–84.

55 Pedersen SS, Kupper N, van Domburg RT. Heart and mind: Are we closer to disentangling the relationship between emotions and poor prognosis in heart disease? *Eur Heart J* 2011;32:2341–3.

56 Wachen JS, Patidar SM, Mulligan EA, et al. Cancer-related PTSD symptoms in a veteran sample: association with age, combat PTSD, and quality of life. *Psycho-Oncology* 2014;23:921–7.

57 Hellmuth JC, Stappenbeck CA, Hoerster KD, Jakupcak M. Modeling PTSD symptom clusters, alcohol misuse, anger, and depression as they relate to aggression and suicidality in returning U.S. veterans. *Journal of Traumatic Stress* 2012;25:527–34.

58 Kendler KS, Neale MC, Kessler RC, et al. The genetic epidemiology of phobias in women: The interrelationship of agoraphobia, social phobia, situational phobia, and simple phobia. *Archives of General Psychiatry* 1992;49:273–81.

59 Horwitz AV. Book review. *New England Journal of Medicine* 2009; 360:841–4.

60 Clarke DJ. The role of multidisciplinary team care in stroke rehabilitation. *Progress in Neurology and Psychiatry* 2013;17:5–8.

61 Intercollegiate Stroke Working Party. *National Clinical Guideline for Stroke*, fourth edition. London: Royal College of Physicians, 2012. Available at: <www.rcplondon.ac.uk/sites/default/files/national -clinical-guidelines-for-stroke-fourth-edition.pdf> [accessed April 2015].

62 Lippman SM, Hawk ET. Cancer Prevention: From 1727 to milestones of the past 100 years. *Cancer Research* 2009;69:5269–84.

63 Lopez-Munoz F, Alamo C. Monoaminergic neurotransmission: The history of the discovery of antidepressants from 1950s until today. *Current Pharmaceutical Design* 2009;15:1563–86.

64 Li J. *Block-Buster Drugs: The Rise and Decline of the Pharmaceutical Industry*, first edition. Oxford University Press, 2014.

65 Cordes E. *Hallelujah Moments: Tales of Drug Discovery*, first edition. Oxford University Press, 2014.

66 Lundh A, Sismondo S, Lexchin J, et al. Industry sponsorship and research outcome. *The Cochrane Database of Systematic Reviews*, 2012;12:MR000033.

67 Turner EH, Matthews AM, Linardatos E, et al. Selective publication of antidepressant trials and its influence on apparent efficacy. *New England Journal of Medicine* 2008;358:252–60.

68 Burdett TC, Freeman MR. Astrocytes eyeball axonal mitochondria. *Science* 2014;345:385–6.

69 Villain M, Segnarbieux F, Bonnel F, et al. The trochlear nerve: Anatomy by microdissection. *Surg Radiol Anat* 1993;15:169–73.

70 Schatzberg AF. Pharmacological principles of antidepressant efficacy. *Human Psychopharmacology: Clinical and Experimental* 2002;17:S17–S22.

71 Greener M. Awareness of interactions has come a long way in 50 years. *Pharmacy Magazine* 2014;September:14.

72 Gray SL, Anderson ML, Dublin S, et al. Cumulative use of strong anticholinergics and incident dementia: A prospective cohort study. *JAMA Internal Medicine* 2015;175:401–407.

73 Lopez-Gonzalez E, Herdeiro MT, Figueiras A. Determinants of under-reporting of adverse drug reactions: A systematic review. *Drug Safety* 2009;32:19–31.

74 Brink CB, Harvey BH, Brand L. Tianeptine: A novel atypical anti-depressant that may provide new insights into the biomolecular basis of depression. *Recent Patents on CNS Drug Discovery* 2006;1:29–41.

75 Lacasse JR, Leo J. Serotonin and depression: A disconnect between the advertisements and the scientific literature. *PLoS Medicine* 2005;2:e392.

76 Gibbons RD, Brown C, Hur K, et al. Suicidal thoughts and behavior with antidepressant treatment: Reanalysis of the randomized placebo-controlled studies of fluoxetine and venlafaxine. *Archives of General Psychiatry* 2012;69:580–7.

77 Fergusson D, Doucette S, Glass KC, et al. Association between suicide attempts and selective serotonin reuptake inhibitors: Systematic review of randomised controlled trials. *British Medical Journal* 2005;330:396.

78 Miller M, Swanson SA, Azrael D, et al. Antidepressant dose, age, and the risk of deliberate self-harm. *JAMA Internal Medicine* 2014;174:899–909.

79 Wall P. Pain and the placebo response. *Ciba Foundation Symposium* 1993;174:187–211.

80 Dorn SD, Kaptchuk TJ, Park JB, et al. A meta-analysis of the placebo response in complementary and alternative medicine trials of irritable bowel syndrome. *Neurogastroenterol Motil* 2007;19:630–7.

81 Diener HC, Bussone G, de Liano H, et al. Placebo-controlled comparison of effervescent acetylsalicylic acid, sumatriptan and ibuprofen in the treatment of migraine attacks. *Cephalalgia* 2004;24:947–54.

82 Servick K. Outsmarting the placebo effect. *Science* 2014;345:1446–7.

83 Colloca L, Miller FG. The nocebo effect and its relevance for clinical practice. *Psychosomatic Medicine* 2011;2011:598–603.

84 Rief W, Nestoriuc Y, von Lilienfeld-Toal A, et al. Differences in adverse effect reporting in placebo groups in SSRI and tricyclic antidepressant trials. *Drug Safety* 2009;32:1041–56.

85 Buoli M, Cumerlato Melter C, Caldiroli A, Altamura AC. Are anti-depressants equally effective in the long-term treatment of major depressive disorder? *Human Psychopharmacology: Clinical and Experimental* 2015;30:21–7.

86 Jeong H-G, Ko Y-H, Oh S-Y, Han C, et al. Effect of Korean Red Ginseng as an adjuvant treatment for women with residual symptoms of major depression. *Asia-Pacific Psychiatry* 2015. DOI:10.1111/appy.12169.

87 Greener M. Beyond serotonin: New approaches to the management of depression. *Progress in Neurology and Psychiatry* 2013;17:23–5.

88 Marston L, Nazareth I, Petersen I, et al. Prescribing of antipsychotics in UK primary care: A cohort study. *BMJ Open* 2014;4.

89 Hoge EA, Ivkovic A, Fricchione GL. Generalized anxiety disorder: Diagnosis and treatment. *BMJ* 2012;345.

90 Baldwin DS, Aitchison K, Bateson A, et al. Benzodiazepines: Risks and benefits. A reconsideration. *Journal of Psychopharmacology* 2013;27:967–71.

91 Banks GP, Mikell CB, Youngerman BE, et al. Neuroanatomical characteristics associated with response to dorsal anterior cingulotomy for obsessive-compulsive disorder. *JAMA Psychiatry* 2015;72:127–35.

92 Dugan DO. Laughter and tears: Best medicine for stress. *Nursing Forum* 1989;24:18–26.

93 Lilienfeld S, Arkowitz H. Are all psychotherapies created equal? *Scientific American Mind* 2012;23. Available at: <www.scientific american.com/article/are-all-psychotherapies-created-equal> [accessed April 2015].

94 Mostofsky E, Penner EA, Mittleman MA. Outbursts of anger as a trigger of acute cardiovascular events: A systematic review and meta-analysis. *European Heart Journal* 2014;35:1404–10.

95 Bateson M, Brilot B, Nettle D. Anxiety: An evolutionary approach. *Can J Psychiatry* 2011;56:707–15.

96 Wiles N, Thomas L, Abel A, et al. Cognitive behavioural therapy as an adjunct to pharmacotherapy for primary care based patients with treatment resistant depression: Results of the CoBalT randomised controlled trial. *The Lancet* 2013;381:375–84.

97 Gould J. Mental health: Stressed students reach out for help. *Nature* 2014;512:223–4.

98 Singh A. Use of mindfulness-based therapies in psychiatry. *Progress in Neurology and Psychiatry* 2012;16:7–11.

99 Robins JLW, Kiken L, Holt M, McCain NL. Mindfulness: An effective coaching tool for improving physical and mental health. *Journal of the American Association of Nurse Practitioners* 2014;26:511–8.

100 Dewi Rees W. The hallucinations of widowhood. *British Medical Journal* 1971;4:37–41.

101 APA (American Psychiatric Association) *Diagnostic and Statistical Manual of Mental Disorders*, fifth edition. Washington DC, 2013.

102 Shear M, Wang Y, Skritskaya N, et al. Treatment of complicated grief in elderly persons: A randomized clinical trial. *JAMA Psychiatry* 2014;71(11):1287–95.

103 Bower B. DSM-5 enters the diagnostic fray: Fifth edition of the widely used psychiatric manual focuses attention on how mental disorders should be defined. *Science News* 2013;183:5–6.

104 Williams C, Wilson P, Morrison J, et al. Guided self-help cognitive behavioural therapy for depression in primary care: A randomised controlled trial. *PLoS ONE* 2013;8:e52735.

105 Krusche A, Cyhlarova E, Williams JMG. Mindfulness online: An evaluation of the feasibility of a web-based mindfulness course for stress, anxiety and depression. *BMJ Open* 2013;3.

106 Davies BE, Morriss R, Glazebrook C. Computer-delivered and web-based interventions to improve depression, anxiety, and psychological well-being of university students: A systematic review and meta-analysis. *J Med Internet Res* 2014;16:e130.

107 Mlyniec K, Davies CL, de Agüero Sánchez IG, et al. Essential elements in depression and anxiety. Part I. *Pharmacological Reports* 2014;66:534–44.

108 Bryson B. *At Home*. Doubleday, 2010.

109 Tolmunen T, Hintikka J, Ruusunen A, et al. Dietary folate and the risk of depression in Finnish middle-aged men. *Psychotherapy and Psychosomatics* 2004;73:334–9.

110 Sarris J, Logan AC, Akbaraly TN, et al. Nutritional medicine as mainstream in psychiatry. *The Lancet Psychiatry* 2015.

111 Su K-P, Lai H-C, Yang H-T, et al. Omega-3 fatty acids in the prevention of interferon-alpha-induced depression: Results from a randomized, controlled trial. *Biological Psychiatry* 2014;76:559–66.

112 Toeller M. Lifestyle Issues: diet. In: Holt RI, Cockram C, Flyvberg A, Goldstein BJ, editors. *Textbook of Diabetes*. Wiley-Blackwell, 2010:346–57.

113 Montgomery GH, Schnur JB, Kravits K. Hypnosis for cancer care: Over 200 years young. *CA: A Cancer Journal for Clinicians* 2013;63:31–44.

114 Abraham HD, Fava M. Order of onset of substance abuse and depression in a sample of depressed outpatients. *Comprehensive Psychiatry* 1999;40:44–50.

115 Robinson J, Sareen J, Cox BJ, Bolton J. Self-medication of anxiety disorders with alcohol and drugs: Results from a nationally representative sample. *Journal of Anxiety Disorders* 2009;23:38–45.

116 Parkin DM. Tobacco-attributable cancer burden in the UK in 2010. *Br J Cancer* 2011;105:S6–S13.

117 Peters SAE, Huxley RR, Woodward M. Smoking as a risk factor for stroke in women compared with men: A systematic review and meta-analysis of 81 cohorts, including 3,980,359 individuals and 42,401 strokes. *Stroke* 2013;44:2821–8.

118 Clancy N, Zwar N, Richmond R. Depression, smoking and smoking cessation: A qualitative study. *Family Practice* 2013;30:587–92.

119 Jiang F, Li S, Pan L, et al. Association of anxiety disorders with the risk of smoking behaviors: A meta-analysis of prospective observational studies. *Drug & Alcohol Dependence* 2014;145:69–76.

120 Taylor G, McNeill A, Girling A, et al. Change in mental health after smoking cessation: Systematic review and meta-analysis. *BMJ* 2014;348:g1151.

121 Semple S, Apsley A, Azmina Ibrahim T, et al. Fine particulate matter concentrations in smoking households: Just how much secondhand smoke do you breathe in if you live with a smoker who smokes indoors? *Tobacco Control* 2014. DOI: doi:10.1136/tobaccocontrol-2014-051635.

122 Lechner WV, Meier E, Wiener JL, et al. The comparative efficacy of 1st vs 2nd generation electronic cigarettes in reducing symptoms of nicotine withdrawal. *Addiction* 2015;110:862–7.

123 McRobbie H, Bullen C, Hartmann-Boyce J, Hajek P. Electronic cigarettes for smoking cessation and reduction. *Cochrane Database of Systematic Reviews* 2014, Wiley Online Library. DOI: 10.1002/14651858. CD010216.pub2.

124 Callahan-Lyon P. Electronic cigarettes: Human health effects. *Tobacco Control* 2014;23:ii36–ii40.

125 Boschloo L, Vogelzangs N, van den Brink W, et al. Depressive and anxiety disorders predicting first incidence of alcohol use disorders: Results of the Netherlands Study of Depression and Anxiety (NESDA). *The Journal of Clinical Psychiatry* 2013;74:1233–40.

126 Boschloo L, Vogelzangs N, van den Brink W, et al. Predictors of the 2-year recurrence and persistence of alcohol dependence. *Addiction* 2012;107:1639–40.

127 Gramenzi A, Caputo F, Biselli M, et al. Alcoholic liver disease – pathophysiological aspects and risk factors. *Alimentary Pharmacology & Therapeutics* 2006;24:1151–61.

128 van Boekel LC, Brouwers EPM, van Weeghel J, Garretsen HFL. Stigma among health professionals towards patients with substance use disorders and its consequences for healthcare delivery: Systematic review. *Drug and Alcohol Dependence* 2013;131:23–35.

129 Conway D. *The Magic of Herbs*. Jonathan Cape, 1973.

130 Ruusunen A, Lehto SM, Tolmunen T, et al. Coffee, tea and caffeine intake and the risk of severe depression in middle-aged Finnish men: The Kuopio Ischaemic Heart Disease Risk Factor Study. *Public Health Nutrition* 2010;13:1215–20.

131 Szpak A, Allen D. A case of acute suicidality following excessive caffeine intake. *Journal of Psychopharmacology* 2012;26:1502–10.

132 Veleber DM, Templer DI. Effects of caffeine on anxiety and depression. *Journal of Abnormal Psychology* 1984;93:120–2.

133 Larsson SC. Coffee, tea, and cocoa and risk of stroke. *Stroke* 2014;45:309–14.

134 Armstrong LE, Ganio MS, Casa DJ, et al. Mild dehydration affects mood in healthy young women. *The Journal of Nutrition* 2012;142:382–8.

135 Ganio MS, Armstrong LE, Casa DJ, et al. Mild dehydration impairs cognitive performance and mood of men. *British Journal of Nutrition* 2011;106:1535–43.

136 Ulrich R. View through a window may influence recovery from surgery. *Science* 1984;224:420–1.

137 Park B, Tsunetsugu Y, Kasetani T, et al. The physiological effects of Shinrin-yoku (taking in the forest atmosphere or forest bathing): Evidence from field experiments in 24 forests across Japan. *Environ Health Prev Med* 2010;15:18–26.

138 Takayama N, Korpela K, Lee J, et al. Emotional, restorative and vitalizing effects of forest and urban environments at four sites in Japan. *International Journal of Environmental Research and Public Health* 2014;11:7207–30.

139 Blumenthal JA, Babyak MA, Doraiswamy PM, et al. Exercise and pharmacotherapy in the treatment of major depressive disorder. *Psychosomatic Medicine* 2007;69:587–96.

140 Sheldrake P. *Spirituality: A Very Short Introduction*. Oxford: Oxford University Press, 2012.

141 Fingelkurts AA. Is our brain hardwired to produce God, or is our brain hardwired to perceive God? A systematic review on the role of the brain in mediating religious experience. *Cognitive Processing* 2009;10:293–326.

142 Polkinghorne J. *Exploring Reality*. London: SPCK, 2005.

143 Koenig HG, Berk LS, Daher NS, et al. Religious involvement is associated with greater purpose, optimism, generosity and gratitude in persons with major depression and chronic medical illness. *Journal of Psychosomatic Research* 2014;77:135–43.

144 Amit BH, Krivoy A, Mansbach-Kleinfeld I, et al. Religiosity is a protective factor against self-injurious thoughts and behaviors in Jewish adolescents: Findings from a nationally representative survey. *European Psychiatry* 2014;29:509–13.

145 Barton YA, Miller L, Wickramaratne P, et al. Religious attendance and social adjustment as protective against depression: A 10-year prospective study. *Journal of Affective Disorders* 2013;146:53–7.

146 Stanley MA, Bush AL, Camp ME, et al. Older adults' preferences for religion/spirituality in treatment for anxiety and depression. *Aging & Mental Health* 2011;15:334–43.

147 Paukert AL, Phillips L, Cully JA, et al. Integration of religion into cognitive-behavioral therapy for geriatric anxiety and depression. *Journal of Psychiatric Practice* 2009;15:103–12.

148 Burkhart L, Schmidt L, Hogan N. Development and psychometric testing of the Spiritual Care Inventory instrument. *Journal of Advanced Nursing* 2011;67:2463–72.

149 King M, Marston L, McManus S, et al. Religion, spirituality and mental health: Results from a national study of English households. *The British Journal of Psychiatry* 2013;202:68–73.

150 Robinson EA, Krentzman AR, Webb JR, Brower KJ. Six-month changes in spirituality and religiousness in alcoholics predict drinking outcomes at nine months. *Journal of Studies on Alcohol and Drugs* 2011;72:660–8.

151 Mueller PS, Plevak DJ, Rummans TA. Religious involvement, spirituality, and medicine: Implications for clinical practice. *Mayo Clinic Proceedings* 2001;76:1225–35.

152 Park C, Dornelas E. Is religious coping related to better quality of life following acute myocardial infarction? *J Relig Health* 2012;51:1337–46.

153 Ong AD, Bergeman CS, Boker SM. Resilience comes of age: Defining features in later adulthood. *Journal of Personality* 2009;77:1777–804.

154 Franks MM, Stephens MA, Rook KS, et al. Spouses' provision of health-related support and control to patients participating in cardiac rehabilitation. *Journal of Family Psychology* 2006;20:311–18.

155 Matuszek S. Animal-facilitated therapy in various patient populations: Systematic literature review. *Holistic Nursing Practice* 2010;24:187–203.

156 Vickers AJ, Cronin AM, Maschino AC, et al. Acupuncture for chronic pain: Individual patient data meta-analysis. *Archives of Internal Medicine* 2012;172:1444–53.

157 MacPherson H, Richmond S, Bland M, et al. Acupuncture and counselling for depression in primary care: A randomised controlled trial. *PLoS Medicine* 2013;10:e1001518.

158 Cooley K, Szczurko O, Perri D, et al. Naturopathic Care for Anxiety: A Randomized Controlled Trial ISRCTN78958974. *PLoS ONE* 2009; 4:e6628.

159 Park C. Mind-body CAM interventions: Current status and considerations for integration into clinical health psychology. *Journal of Clinical Psychology* 2013;69:45–63.

160 Goes TC, Antunes FD, Alves PB, Teixeira-Silva F. Effect of sweet orange aroma on experimental anxiety in humans. *Journal of Alternative and Complementary Medicine* 2012;18:798–804.

161 Anon. The discussion on hypnotism. *British Medical Journal* 1890;1:1259–70.

162 Bivins R. *Alternative Medicine? A History.* Oxford University Press, 2007.

163 Donesky-Cuenco D, Nguyen HQ, Paul S, Carrieri-Kohlman V. Yoga therapy decreases dyspnea-related distress and improves functional performance in people with chronic obstructive pulmonary disease: A pilot study. *Journal of Alternative and Complementary Medicine* 2009;15:225–34.

164 Cramer H, Lauche R, Hohmann C, et al. Yoga for chronic neck pain: A 12-month follow-up. *Pain Medicine* 2013;14:541–8.

165 Streeter C, Whitfield T, Owen L, et al. Effects of yoga versus walking on mood, anxiety, and brain GABA levels: A randomized controlled MRS study. *Journal of Alternative and Complementary Medicine* 2010;16:1145–52.

166 Ross A, Friedmann E, Bevans M, Thomas S. Frequency of yoga practice predicts health: Results of a national survey of yoga practitioners. *Evidence-Based Complementary and Alternative Medicine* 2012;2012:10.

167 Krief S, Jamart A, Mahé S, et al. Clinical and pathologic manifestation of oesophagostomosis in African great apes: Does self-medication in wild apes influence disease progression? *Journal of Medical Primatology* 2008;37:188–95.

168 Linde K, Berner M, Levente K. St John's wort for major depression. *Cochrane Database of Systematic Reviews*, 2008, Wiley Online Library. DOI:10.1002/14651858.CD000448.pub3.

169 Russo E, Scicchitano F, Whalley BJ, et al. Hypericum perforatum: Pharmacokinetic, mechanism of action, tolerability, and clinical drug–drug interactions. *Phytotherapy Research* 2014;28:643–55.

170 Davis SA, Feldman SR, Taylor SL. Use of St. John's wort in potentially dangerous combinations. *The Journal of Alternative and Complementary Medicine* 2014;20:578–9.

171 Ernst E. Risks of herbal medicinal products. *Pharmacoepidemiology and Drug Safety* 2004;13:767–71.

172 Sarris J, Stough C, Bousman CA, et al. Kava in the treatment of generalized anxiety disorder: A double-blind, randomized, placebo-controlled study. *Journal of Clinical Psychopharmacology* 2013;33:643–8.

173 Lam RW. Sleep disturbances and depression: A challenge for anti-depressants. *International Clinical Psychopharmacology* 2006;21:S25–S29.

174 Takeda M, Hashimoto R, Kudo T, et al. Laughter and humor as complementary and alternative medicines for dementia patients. *BMC Complementary and Alternative Medicine* 2010;10:28.

175 Mora-Ripoll R. The therapeutic value of laughter in medicine. *Alternative Therapies in Health and Medicine* 2010;16:56–64.

176 Tacchi M, Scott J. *Depression: A Very Short Introduction.* Oxford University Press, 2017.

177 Foster R, Kreitzman L. *Circadian Rhythms: A Very Short Introduction.* Oxford University Press, 2017.

178 Ravindran AV, Balneaves LG, Faulkner G, et al. Canadian Network for Mood Anxiety Treatment (CANMAT) 2016 clinical guidelines for the management of adults with major depressive disorder: Section 5.

Complementary and alternative medicine treatments. *The Canadian Journal of Psychiatry* 2016;61:576–87.

179 Freeman D, Freeman J. *Anxiety: A Very Short Introduction.* Oxford University Press, 2012.

180 Greener M. Bullying and mental health – the risk factors and legacy. *Progress in Neurology and Psychiatry* 2015;19:11–13.

181 Greener M. Understanding the long-term effects of bullying. *British Journal of School Nursing* 2016;11:36–9.

182 O'Shea M. *The Brain: A Very Short Introduction.* Oxford University Press, 2005.

183 Aalbers S, Fusar-Poli L, Freeman RE, et al. Music therapy for depression. *Cochrane Database of Systematic Reviews,* 2017;11:CD004517.

184 Butler G, McManus F. *Psychology: A Very Short Introduction,* second edition. Oxford University Press, 2014.

185 Blanck P, Perleth S, Heidenreich T, et al. Effects of mindfulness exercises as stand-alone intervention on symptoms of anxiety and depression: Systematic review and meta-analysis. *Behaviour Research and Therapy* 2018;102:25–35.

186 Zhang A, Park S, Sullivan JE, et al. The effectiveness of problem-solving therapy for primary care patients' depressive and/or anxiety disorders: A systematic review and meta-analysis. *The Journal of the American Board of Family Medicine* 2018;31:139–50.

187 Gilman SE, Sucha E, Kingsbury M, et al. Depression and mortality in a longitudinal study: 1952–2011. *Canadian Medical Association Journal* 2017;189:E1304–E1310.

188 Lowe NM, Bhojani I. Special consideration for vitamin D in the south Asian population in the UK. *Therapeutic Advances in Musculoskeletal Disease* 2017;9:137–44.

189 NICE. Vitamin D: Supplement use in specific population groups. London: NICE, 2017. Available at <www.nice.org.uk/guidance/ph56> [accessed January 2018].

190 Vernocchi P, Del Chierico F, Putignani L. Gut microbiota profiling: Metabolomics based approach to unravel compounds affecting human health. *Frontiers in Microbiology* 2016;7. DOI:10.3389/fmicb.2016.01144.

191 Spanogiannopoulos P, Bess EN, Carmody RN, et al. The microbial pharmacists within us: A metagenomic view of xenobiotic metabolism. *Nature Reviews: Microbiology* 2016;14:273–87.

192 Cenit M, Sanz Y, Codoñer-Franch P. Influence of gut microbiota on neuropsychiatric disorders. *World J Gastroenterol* 2017;23:5486–98.

193 Sherwin E, Dinan T, Cryan J. Recent developments in understanding the role of the gut microbiota in brain health and disease. *Annals of the New York Academy of Sciences* 2017. DOJ:10.1111/nyas.13416.

194 Allen AP, Hutch W, Borre YE, et al. *Bifidobacterium longum* 1714 as a translational psychobiotic: Modulation of stress, electrophysiology and neurocognition in healthy volunteers. *Transl Psychiatry* 2016;6:e939.

195 Steenbergen L, Sellaro R, van Hemert S, et al. A randomized controlled trial to test the effect of multispecies probiotics on cognitive reactivity

to sad mood. *Brain, Behavior, and Immunity* 2015;48:258–64.

196 Kelly JR, Borre Y, O'Brien C, et al. Transferring the blues: Depression-associated gut microbiota induces neurobehavioural changes in the rat. *Journal of Psychiatric Research* 2016;82:109–18.

197 Keefe JR, Mao JJ, Soeller I, et al. Short-term open-label chamomile (*Matricaria chamomilla* L.) therapy of moderate to severe generalized anxiety disorder. *Phytomedicine* 2016;23:1699–705.

198 Ng QX, Venkatanarayanan N, and Ho CYX. Clinical use of *Hypericum perforatum* (St John's wort) in depression: A meta-analysis. *Journal of Affective Disorders* 2017;210:211–21.

199 Lockley S, Foster R. *Sleep: A Very Short Introduction*. Oxford University Press, 2012.

200 DeWall CN, MacDonald G, Webster GD, et al. Acetaminophen reduces social pain: Behavioral and neural evidence. *Psychological Science* 2010;21:931–7.

201 Kross E, Berman MG, Mischel W, et al. Social rejection shares somatosensory representations with physical pain. *Proceedings of the National Academy of Sciences* 2011;108:6270–5.

202 Read J, Cartwright C and Gibson K. How many of 1829 antidepressant users report withdrawal effects or addiction? *International Journal of Mental Health Nursing* 2018. DOI:10.1111/inm.12488.

203 Hendriks T. The effects of Sahaja Yoga meditation on mental health: A systematic review. *Journal of Complementary and Integrative Medicine* 2018. DOI:10.1515/jcim-2016-016.

204 Johnson D, Dupuis G, Piche J, et al. Adult mental health outcomes of adolescent depression: A systematic review. *Depression and Anxiety* 2018. DOI:10.1002/da.22777.

205 Schaakxs R, Comijs HC, Lamers F, et al. Associations between age and the course of major depressive disorder: A 2-year longitudinal cohort study. *The Lancet Psychiatry* 2018. DOI:10.1016/S2215-0366(18)30166–4.

206 Qota DM, Ozenberger K and Olfson M. Prevalence of prescription medications with depression as a potential adverse effect among adults in the United States. *JAMA* 2018;319:2289–8.

207 Gordon BR, McDowell CP, Hallgren M, et al. Association of efficacy of resistance exercise training with depressive symptoms: Meta-analysis and meta-regression analysis of randomized clinical trials. *JAMA Psychiatry* 2018;75:566–76.

208 Cipriani A, Furukawa TA, Salanti G, et al. Comparative efficacy and acceptability of 21 antidepressant drugs for the acute treatment of adults with major depressive disorder: A systematic review and network meta-analysis. *The Lancet* 2018;391:1357–66.

Further reading

Bender, DA. *Nutrition: A very short introduction*. Oxford University Press, 2014.

Bivins, Roberta. *Alternative Medicine? A History*. Oxford University Press, 2007.

Butler, G and McManus, F. *Psychology: A very short introduction*, second edition. Oxford University Press, 2014.

Cantopher, Tim. *Depressive Illness: The curse of the strong*. London: Sheldon Press, 2012.

Freeman, D and Freeman, J. *Anxiety: A very short introduction*. Oxford University Press, 2012.

Greener, Mark. *Coping with Liver Disease*. London: Sheldon Press, 2013.

Greener, Mark. *Coping with Thyroid Disease*. London: Sheldon Press, 2014.

Greener, Mark. *The Heart Attack Survival Guide*. London: Sheldon Press, 2012.

Greener, Mark. *The Holistic Health Handbook*. London: Sheldon Press, 2013.

Greener, Mark. *The Which? Guide To Managing Stress*, second edition. London: Which? Books, 2002.

Greener, Mark. *The Which? Way To Manage Your Time – And Your Life*. London: Which? Books, 2000.

Harrington, Anne. *The Cure Within: A history of mind–body medicine*. New York: W.W. Norton, 2008.

Kirsch, Irving. *The Emperor's New Drugs: Exploding the antidepressant myth*. Bodley Head, 2009.

Mabey, Richard. *Nature Cure*. Vintage Press, 2008.

O'Shea, M. *The Brain: A very short introduction*. Oxford University Press, 2005.

Otto, Michael W. and Smits, Jasper A. J. *Exercise for Mood and Anxiety: Proven strategies for overcoming depression and enhancing well-being*. Oxford University Press, 2011.

Rowe, Dorothy. *Depression: The way out of your prison*, second edition. Routledge, 1996.

Russell, Andrew. *The Social Basis of Medicine*, first edition. Oxford: Wiley-Blackwell, 2009.

Sheldrake, Philip. *Spirituality: A very short introduction*. Oxford University Press, 2012.

Showalter, Elaine. *Hystories: Hysterical epidemics and modern culture*. Picador, 1998.

Smith, Katharine. *Recovering from Depression: A companion guide for Christians*. SPCK, 2014.

Strohecker, James, Strohecker, Nancy Shaw and Bresler, David, editors. *Natural Healing for Depression*. Perigee Books, 1999.

Styron, William. *Darkness Visible: A memoir of madness*. Jonathan Cape, 1991.

Tacchi, MJ and Scott, J. *Depression: A very short introduction*. Oxford University Press, 2017.

Tallis, Frank. *How To Stop Worrying*, second edition. London: Sheldon Press, 2014.

Index

Overcoming Common Problems Series

Selected titles

A full list of titles is available from Sheldon Press,
36 Causton Street, London SW1P 4ST and on our website at
www.sheldonpress.co.uk

The A to Z of Eating Disorders
Emma Woolf

Autism and Asperger Syndrome in Adults
Dr Luke Beardon

Beating Insomnia: Without really trying
Dr Tim Cantopher

Birth Over 35
Sheila Kitzinger

Breast Cancer: Your treatment choices
Dr Terry Priestman

Bulimia, Binge-eating and Their Treatment
Professor J. Hubert Lacey, Dr Bryony Bamford .
and Amy Brown

The Chronic Fatigue Healing Diet
Christine Craggs-Hinton

**Chronic Fatigue Syndrome: What you need
to know about CFS/ME**
Dr Megan A. Arroll

The Chronic Pain Diet Book
Neville Shone

Chronic Pain the Drug-free Way
Phil Sizer

Cider Vinegar
Margaret Hills

Coeliac Disease: What you need to know
Alex Gazzola

**Coping Successfully with Chronic Illness:
Your healing plan**
Neville Shone

Coping Successfully with Hiatus Hernia
Dr Tom Smith

Coping Successfully with Pain
Neville Shone

Coping Successfully with Panic Attacks
Shirley Trickett

Coping Successfully with Shyness
Margaret Oakes, Professor Robert Bor
and Dr Carina Eriksen

Coping Successfully with Ulcerative Colitis
Peter Cartwright

**Coping with a Mental Health Crisis:
Seven steps to healing**
Catherine G. Lucas

Coping with Aggressive Behaviour
Dr Jane McGregor

Coping with Bronchitis and Emphysema
Dr Tom Smith

Coping with Diverticulitis
Peter Cartwright

Coping with Endometriosis
Jill Eckersley and Dr Zara Aziz

Coping with Epilepsy
Dr Pamela Crawford and Fiona Marshall

Coping with Gout
Christine Craggs-Hinton

Coping with Headaches and Migraine
Alison Frith

Coping with Liver Disease
Mark Greener

Coping with Memory Problems
Dr Sallie Baxendale

Coping with Phobias and Panic
Professor Kevin Gournay

Coping with Schizophrenia
Professor Kevin Gournay and Debbie Robson

Coping with Stomach Ulcers
Dr Tom Smith

**Coping with the Psychological Effects of
Cancer**
Professor Robert Bor, Dr Carina Eriksen
and Ceilidh Stapelkamp

Coping with the Psychological Effects of Illness
Dr Fran Smith, Dr Carina Eriksen
and Professor Robert Bor

Dementia Care: A guide
Christina Macdonald

Overcoming Common Problems Series

Depression and Anxiety the Drug-free Way
Mark Greener

Depressive Illness: The curse of the strong
Dr Tim Cantopher

Dr Dawn's Guide to Brain Health
Dr Dawn Harper

Dr Dawn's Guide to Digestive Health
Dr Dawn Harper

Dr Dawn's Guide to Healthy Eating for Diabetes
Dr Dawn Harper

Dr Dawn's Guide to Healthy Eating for IBS
Dr Dawn Harper

Dr Dawn's Guide to Heart Health
Dr Dawn Harper

Dr Dawn's Guide to Sexual Health
Dr Dawn Harper

Dr Dawn's Guide to Weight and Diabetes
Dr Dawn Harper

Dr Dawn's Guide to Women's Health
Dr Dawn Harper

Dr Dawn's Guide to Your Baby's First Year
Dr Dawn Harper

Dr Dawn's Guide to Toddler Health
Dr Dawn Harper

Dying for a Drink: All you need to know to beat the booze
Dr Tim Cantopher

The Empathy Trap: Understanding antisocial personalities
Dr Jane McGregor and Tim McGregor

Epilepsy: Complementary and alternative treatments
Dr Sallie Baxendale

Everything Your GP Doesn't Have Time to Tell You about Arthritis
Dr Matt Piccaver

Fibromyalgia: Your treatment guide
Christine Craggs-Hinton

The Fibromyalgia Healing Diet
Christine Craggs-Hinton

Gestational Diabetes: Your survival guide to diabetes in pregnancy
Dr Paul Grant

Hay Fever: How to beat it
Dr Paul Carson

The Heart Attack Survival Guide
Mark Greener

The Holistic Guide for Cancer Survivors
Mark Greener

How to Accept Yourself
Dr Windy Dryden

How to Beat Worry and Stress
Dr David Delvin

How to Eat Well When You Have Cancer
Jane Freeman

How to Stop Worrying
Dr Frank Tallis

IBS: Dietary advice to calm your gut
Alex Gazzola and Julie Thompson

The Irritable Bowel Diet Book
Rosemary Nicol

Jealousy: Why it happens and how to overcome it
Dr Paul Hauck

Living with Angina
Dr Tom Smith

Living with Fibromyalgia
Christine Craggs-Hinton

Living with Hearing Loss
Dr Don McFerran, Lucy Handscomb and Dr Cherilee Rutherford

Living with Multiple Sclerosis
Mark Greener

Living with the Challenges of Dementia: A guide for family and friends
Patrick McCurry

Living with Tinnitus and Hyperacusis
Dr Laurence McKenna, Dr David Baguley and Dr Don McFerran

Losing a Parent
Fiona Marshall

Menopause: The drug-free way
Dr Julia Bressan

Mental Health in Children and Young People: Spotting symptoms and seeking help early
Dr Sarah Vohra

Motor Neurone Disease: A family affair
Dr David Oliver

The Multiple Sclerosis Diet Book
Tessa Buckley

Overcoming Common Problems Series

Overcome Your Fear of Flying
Professor Robert Bor, Dr Carina Eriksen
and Margaret Oakes

Overcoming Anxiety
Dr Windy Dryden

Overcoming Emotional Abuse
Susan Elliot-Wright

Overcoming Fear with Mindfulness
Deborah Ward

**Overcoming Gambling: A guide for problem
and compulsive gamblers**
Philip Mawer

Overcoming Jealousy
Dr Windy Dryden

Overcoming Low Self-esteem with Mindfulness
Deborah Ward

Overcoming Stress
Professor Robert Bor, Dr Carina Eriksen
and Dr Sara Chaudry

**The Pain Management Handbook: Your
personal guide**
Neville Shone

The Panic Workbook
Dr Carina Eriksen, Professor Robert Bor
and Margaret Oakes

**Parenting Your Disabled Child: The first three
years**
Margaret Barrett

**Post-Traumatic Stress Disorder: Recovery after
accident and disaster**
Professor Kevin Gournay

Reducing Your Risk of Dementia
Dr Tom Smith

The Self-esteem Journal
Alison Waines

Sleep Better: The science and the myths
Professor Graham Law and Dr Shane Pascoe

Stress-related Illness
Dr Tim Cantopher

The Stroke Survival Guide
Mark Greener

**Taming the Beast Within: Understanding
personality disorder**
Professor Peter Tyrer

Ten Steps to Positive Living
Dr Windy Dryden

Therapy Pets: A guide
Jill Eckersley

**Toxic People: Dealing with dysfunctional
relationships**
Dr Tim Cantopher

**Transforming Eight Deadly Emotions into
Healthy Ones**
Dr Windy Dryden

Treat Your Own Knees
Jim Johnson

Treating Arthritis: The drug-free way
Margaret Hills and Christine Horner

Treating Arthritis: More ways to a drug-free life
Margaret Hills

Treating Arthritis: The supplements guide
Julia Davies

Treating Arthritis Diet Book
Margaret Hills

Treating Arthritis Exercise Book
Margaret Hills and Janet Horwood

Understanding High Blood Pressure
Dr Shahid Aziz and Dr Zara Aziz

Understanding Hoarding
Jo Cooke

Understanding Obsessions and Compulsions
Dr Frank Tallis

**Understanding Yourself and Others: Practical
ideas from the world of coaching**
Bob Thomson

Vertigo and Dizziness
Jaydip Ray

When Someone You Love Has Dementia
Susan Elliot-Wright

**When Someone You Love Has Depression:
A handbook for family and friends**
Barbara Baker

The Whole Person Recovery Handbook
Emma Drew

**Your Guide for the Cancer Journey: Cancer and
its treatment**
Mark Greener

Lists of titles in the Mindful Way and Sheldon Short Guides series are also available from Sheldon Press.